Rotten Minerva

Part One

Be an Unruly Warrior and Embark on a Spiritual Quest

Kelli Hastings

Sister Lotus Yoga LLC, Publisher

ORLANDO, FL

Sister Lotus Yoga, LLC
4005 North Orange Blossom Trail
Orlando, FL 32804
www.sisterlotusyoga.com

Publisher's Note: This book is memoir-ish nonfiction. It reflects the author's present recollections of events and circumstances that occurred in the past. It also contains the author's personal opinions, with which you can freely disagree. The names and some details have been changed to protect privacy, and some events have been compressed and dialogue recreated

Rotten Minerva/ Kelli Hastings -- 1st ed.
ISBN 978-1-7331173-0-2

Table of Contents

On August 21, 2017, all of America came together to gaze upward toward the heavens.

For two minutes, we put politics and disagreements aside and were united to experience the awe of Nature.

We all realized and paid some respect to—whether consciously or unconsciously—a force larger than ourselves.

Hundreds of people, including me, descended upon Branchville, South Carolina, population 900, to experience a clear shot of totality; an unobstructed view of the total eclipse of the sun.

Branchville is the world's oldest railroad junction; the first ever crossroads.

And from that crossroads, all silly distinctions between us put aside for a moment, we witnessed the brief death of the sun; the thing directly responsible for all of life on Earth.

Humankind is at a crossroads.

And that brings me to this book.

It is no meaningless coincidence that this book was completed at the time of the Great American Eclipse. I hope that it will inspire its readers to undertake a journey into themselves; to continue to take brief moments daily to acknowledge the bigness of Nature; and to witness death and change with a newfound sense of freedom.

It is set up in four sections which mirror the four *padas* of Patanjali's Yoga Sutras. The Yoga Sutras will be discussed in more detail in the body of this book.

If yoga isn't your thing, that is cool too. I'm a yogi, so I tend to use yogic terms. If you want to gloss over the yoga terminology, that is ok.[1] The bottom line is that it's not necessary to understand or care about the yoga words to get the gist of this book.

The first section of this book is "Love." It describes my philosophy of life, and is supported by references to sacred writings, science, and my observations.

The second section is "Practice." It outlines the practical means that I undertook on my personal quest for truth and freedom. It is interspersed with humorous stories of my own misadventures on the path.

---

[1] Or feel free to use the *GLOSS*...ary of Yogic Terms on page 173. [*snort-laughs while pushing glasses back up on nose*].

The third section is "Magic," and it sets forth the unexplained magic that might be encountered on the path, including stories of the mysterious and wonderful that I directly experienced on my journey. It also includes a bit of a road map for entering into the shadow and tales of my own tumultuous journey into my cave of darkness.

The last section is "Freedom." It presents the results of undertaking the quest that I hope all my readers will resolve to undertake, and includes some fun stories too. Spoiler alert: the results of undertaking your own personal quest are love, truth, authenticity, and freedom.

Sounds pretty sweet, right?

Let's do it.

I. Love

Ishvara pranidhanat va

"The practice of Devotion brings imminent bliss"

~ Sutra I, 23, <u>The Yoga Sutras of Patanjali</u>

CHAPTER 1

My Story

The cave that you fear holds the treasure you seek.

~ Joseph Campbell

...

Yoda: That place...is strong with the dark side of the Force. A domain of evil it is. In you must go.

Luke: What's in there?

Yoda: Only what you take with you.

~ <u>The Empire Strikes Back</u>

Mine is the classic story of suffering and redemption. It is a story of undertaking a quest and entering into the cave of darkness; of battling elusive tigers and confronting the Dark Side of the Force in order to uncover the hidden treasures of the soul.

In fact, that may seriously be the only story *ever*.

By that I mean, it is definitely arguable that all stories of all time can be boiled down into that specific plot scenario: hero undertakes a journey, enters into the darkness—encounters and defeats monsters or otherwise faces her fears—and recovers the light.

Of course, the darkness, the monsters, the fears—and even the light that is recovered—can take many different forms. But all stories—from the Wizard of Oz, to Star Wars, to Dumb and Dumber, to the Little Engine that Could—conceivably fit that mold.

Why is *that* humanity's one-trick-wonder story?.

Think about it.

I have a theory, but we will let this book speak for itself. My goal is to get you thinking about life a little differently than you did before you picked up this book, and to get you pumped to undertake your own quest and discovery your own story.

So back to *my* story which, remember I said was classic.

And let's face it, this is my book and you are pretty much forced to believe me while you read it.

Or at least suspend disbelief.

Although I suppose you could read the whole book with pursed lips while silently shaking your head in disagreement with everything I say.

(As long as you read it, we're cool...)

So, I grew up in a small town, went to college, then to law school, got a good job as a lawyer, and got married. But deep down, I was not happy. My life was tinged with anxiety and worry, and my mind was constantly racing.

Then, life brought about suffering through the cancer deaths of my Dad and brother, who died six months apart in 2010.

Suffering has a way of waking us up, doesn't it? In fact, many periods of great awakening in history were preceded by periods of great darkness. The Renaissance, for example, followed the Dark Ages.

Humanity is suffering greatly right now. There is political unrest, poverty, terrorism, hatred, disease, and other horrible atrocities which we must face here on Earth *right now*.

The hidden glory in suffering is that it brings freedom through awakening.

Often, our minds are full of imagining the worst things that could happen in our lives. And when one of the worst things that could happen, does happen, fear loses some of its grip.

We start living our lives with less fear.

In other words, if we could live through one of the worst things that we can imagine, and come out on the other side of it okay, then what is there to fear? What is there to do but be our most open authentic selves?

Orlando, my home town, experienced this as a community in the aftermath of the Pulse mass shooting tragedy. I don't think anybody could've imagined something like that happening in our community until it did. Now I see that one of the silver linings to it is that our town really started to tap into that sense of fearlessness.

That sense of, "we are going to proudly be who we are; and no matter what type of hatred or terror comes our way, we're going to continue to rise up as a community and be a force of love and compassion."

That is the awesomeness of tragedy. Suffering brings awakening. We are in a time of great suffering here on earth. And we are on the cusp of great change. Suffering creates space for fearlessness which allows us to live with open hearts even in the face of hate and terror.

But we really don't need any more suffering to tap into that fearlessness—that open-heartedness. We can recognize the drama of suffering for what it is and begin to awaken ourselves to that fearlessness, that love, without the need for additional tragedies and suffering.

I believe we are in the beginning stages of a great awakening, similar to the awakening I experienced on a smaller scale in my own life.

My son was also born in 2010, the year my Dad and Daniel died. It is funny how life works that way. One of the worst years of my life was also one of the best.

I want my son to experience a peaceful, happy life, and I hope he can avoid some of the suffering I experienced. And I do believe it is possible to "wake up" without deep suffering, but we will talk more on that later.

Upon the deaths of Daniel and my Dad, I went inward for answers. I dived deep into my yoga and spiritual practices in search of peace. My journey led me to a small town in southwest India: Mysore, Karnataka.

In Mysore, I was blown away. The people, for the most part, seemed genuinely happy— not like in America. There were lots of people there that had lots of reasons to be unhappy (so I thought) but they really seemed to have found a deep joy.

For example, there was a man with no legs who would hang out every day by the coconut stand begging for money. He got around by walking on his hands with the help of thick blocks attached to his palms. He always had the biggest smile on his face; nodding a toothless greeting of pure joy while offering blessings to all who passed by.

With a hint of annoyance and jealousy I thought, "Why is he so freaking happy?!?"

I came to realize that the people in Mysore were connected with their inner divinity in a way that is not common in the West. In India, everything is worshipped as Divine—from the multitude of different deities, to the plants, to the food, to the *cows*—everything is seen as God expressed in form. I came to see life that way, too, and I'll tell you what—it makes for a much happier existence.

Am I perfect now? Not really, though I guess that depends on your point of view. I have my share of shameless vices, and I live to enjoy life, not deprive myself of it. But I am perfectly myself; and I live my life with authenticity and freedom.

My late grandmother, "Grandma Teddy," used to write and illustrate stories for me and Daniel and our cousins about a young heroine named "Rotten Minerva." Minerva was kind-hearted—but with a naughty streak—she was a little "rotten," as Grandma Teddy would say. Minerva learned life lessons the hard way sometimes. But she always learned from her mistakes, and we always rooted for her.

In a way, this is her story, and I hope you come away from it as a member of Team Minerva, too—ready to undertake your own deeply personal spiritual journey despite the missteps you will likely take along the way.

And, really, are there any missteps in life? I firmly believe that we are here on Earth to learn—I mean, why are we here if not to learn?[2] Everything that happens to us - for good or ill - is part of our journey.'

---

[2] Well, maybe we are also here to enjoy ourselves a bit while we learn. More on Lila, God's play, in the Mermaid Chapter.

CHAPTER 2

So Wait, Back Up, Did You Say God is a Cow?

...the devotees who worship me with love reside in me and I reside in them.
~ Krishna to Arjuna, <u>The Bhagavad Gita</u>

...

Luminous beings are we, not this crude matter.
~ Yoda, <u>The Empire Strikes Back</u>

I'm not saying God is a cow, or that God is anything really.

Or that we should even call It God. That term has developed lots of connotations that don't really apply to my concept of what *It* is.

I like the term "Universe" because it literally means, "one verse" and it invokes the idea of a "song." I like the music metaphor because we are all part of one infinitely beautiful song; one that we can choose to dance and sing to once we tune into its divine beat.

But most often I connect with divinity through the Divine Feminine or the Divine Mother—this idea that all of the manifested world is inherently maternal, feminine energy, that can be felt as warm, motherly Love.

In India, there are so many different depictions of the Divine Mother. I personally love Kali, who is fierce and intense like Mother Nature herself. I tend to be more private about Kali so as not to freak people out - she is often illustrated with severed heads around her neck and is worshipped in cremation grounds. It's symbology[3], folks. But it is also kind of shocking if you are unfamiliar with it.

The Divine Father is cool too. Jesus is the aspect of the Divine Father I feel most connected too, having been raised Catholic. Like the Divine Feminine, fatherly love can be felt as the underlying essential current of all of our material reality. You get to pick your flavor of divinity—or perhaps it picks you. Regardless, you can choose

---

[3] I realize the correct word is "symbolism," but I couldn't resist an obscure nineties movie reference. Contact me for a prize if you guess right.

to worship the Divine in the form that makes the most sense to you and your upbringing. It's ultimately all the same.

In fact, "The Yoga Sutras" teach us that divinity should be worshipped according to your personal religious heritage[4] and your personal concept of the Divine.[5] The Yoga Sutras were written over 2000 years ago by the great sage Patanjali. The Yoga Sutras, along with "The Bhagavad Gita" (also over 2000 years old) set forth the essential teachings of yoga and are must-reads for any serious yoga students.

The phrase "*Ishvara pranidhana*" comes up multiple times in the Sutras and is referenced in the Bhagavad Gita too. It refers to the practice of devotion, also known as *bhakti* yoga. The phrase "*Ishvara pranidhana*" literally means "devotion to Ishvara."

Ishvara can be a personal concept of the Divine, like Jesus, Krishna, the Divine Mother, Kali, Allah, Amma, the Pope, Nature, Ancestors, or any of the millions of other forms through which humans have worshipped Divinity for countless millennia. In this book, I use the terms *bhakti* yoga, *Ishvara pranidhana*, and devotion in-

---

[4] Sutra I, 39 says, "*yatha abhimata dhyanat va*" or "serenity can be found by meditating according to one's religious heritage."

[5] See Sutras I, 23-27; II-1, II, 32, II, 45, which reference the practice of *Ishvara pranidana*.

terchangeably. The key to devotion is to pick the form of the divine that resonates most with you, and then to strive to see that form in all beings and manifestations.

And I mentioned Amma, who is a human being on Earth right now that resonates with me as my guru. She is called "the hugging saint" or the "Indian Mother Teresa." Her *dharma* or divine service is to offer hugs to all who come to see her. She tours the world giving out hugs and doing humanitarian works, often feeding the thousands that come to see her for free. I waited ten (10) hours with my then 2-year old son to get my Amma hug the first time I met her in Mysore. It was well worth it. It was an auspicious, heart-opening experience.

She hugged people for 20 hours straight that day. That is amazing in itself; a sixty-something year old women spending 20-plus hours hugging thousands of people while offering them all free food.[6] She is an amazing human being. She devotes her life to others, with a particular focus on orphaned children. I love Amma.

And Pope Francis, who I mentioned too, is a human being on Earth now that can be a gateway to divinity

---

[6] The food was free when I saw her in India. The times I have seen her in America there was a nominal charge for food, but the hugs and meditation service have always been free. The trade-off is that in America, the wait time is much quicker—more like 2 hours than 10.

through the practice of devotion. I had a particularly auspicious experience in his presence during a trip to Italy, where we were lucky enough—after a series of misadventures—to be in exactly the right place at the exact right time and see him deliver a homily in Vatican Square, as if guided there by my Dad. I love Papa Francesco too.

Yes, they are human beings and subject to the laws of nature and the duality of good and evil that exists in all material forms. But at the same time, they can be living examples of aligning with the divinity within.

There is a documentary called, "Kumare," about a young filmmaker from New Jersey who decides to impersonate his grandmother's Indian accent, grow out his beard, don monk's robes, and act like a guru for the sole purpose of seeing if he can trick people into following him for the documentary he is making. He calls himself Kumare, and hires a few "devotees" to travel with him and act like worshippers as part of the act.

It works; he gains many followers who are truly uplifted by his words and teachings. Kumare was a gateway for these people to have true, heart-opening spiritual experiences, even though he was essentially a fraud.

Kumare then does the "big reveal" and tells them he was basically faking it for the documentary. This is where it gets really interesting: many of his followers stayed with him even after they found out he was "fake," because of what they felt within themselves in his presence. What they learned about themselves was real, even though it came through a false teacher. "Kumare" learned a lesson too, about the nature of Divine Truth.

The point is, when you take up the practice of devotion and open yourself up to the quest, don't be disheartened if your human teachers are not perfect; divinity shines through everyone and a true message can be delivered even through an imperfect messenger. That does not mean that you should not maintain healthy boundaries and use caution; just that it is important to trust the process and the journey.

Nonetheless, based on my personal experience, Amma and Pope Francis are two humans that exist on Earth now that are the real deal. A palpable energetic upliftment can be felt in their presence.

To me, Amma and Pope Francis are vehicles for connecting with the Divine Mother and Father; they are versions of the Divine Parenthood in form on Earth right now that I can look to as symbols of that same divinity inside of me; I can practice devotion with them in mind. Depending on your personal leanings, you might find it is nice to have a person in form on Earth who can be a specific symbol of the divine for you.

Yet there is a benefit to keeping your concept of the divine less specific and more broad, rather than thinking of God as a specific man or woman or super-person.

In other words, if you're concept of God is limited to, for example, Jesus, the man that lived on Earth over 2000 years ago, it may be more difficult to realize that Christ is also your neighbor and the tree in your yard.

And we can agree that having a very specific concept of the divine that is not open to other concepts of divinity has gotten humankind into some trouble in the past.

For that reason and others, I think most of us have become disheartened with the pseudo- Judeo-Christian idea of a grey-haired man in the sky with a beard, which, by the way, isn't really the biblical idea of God at all.

Recall that Jesus said to his disciples, "I am in my Father, and you are in me, and I am in you."[7] That doesn't sound like the concept of a personified God that is apart and separate from us, does it?

Neither does the line from The Bhagavad Gita, quoted at the outset of this chapter, where Krishna [God] tells his devotee, Arjuna, that he "is actually part of [him]" and "lives in [him]."

But before I lose you with ancient scripture, let me lose you with quantum physics.

---

[7] John 14:20.

Let's develop a new idea of what God might be.

Quantum physics teaches us that at the quantum level, we don't really exist. Forgive me for oversimplifying here, but basically, if you look at matter—including the human body—at the smallest most minute level, we are made up of atoms that are made up of even smaller things. When these smaller things are looked at, we see that, first of all, we are almost entirely empty space; and second, we are neither a wave (the movement of energy) nor a particle (matter/material substance). The act of observation decides whether a wave or particle is seen. Lots of quantum physicists have written a great deal on this subject and could do it a lot more justice than I can here.[8]

The important take away is that we really aren't as solid as we appear. At the quantum level, our bodies look more like stars in the night sky than a solid mass because of all the space between the atoms, and the atoms themselves are deceptive because they really aren't solid matter either. And the act of observation itself can have an effect on or otherwise change what we see in our material reality.

---

[8] For more information, Google the "Copenhagen interpretation" or "Schrodinger's Cat."

What does that have to do with God? I'm not sure, but it does point to a reality that isn't exactly what it seems. And what precisely is all that empty space made up of? Perhaps it is the empty space that exists in all things that connects us to one another, and makes us "one verse." And when we are open to the possibility of perceiving all of life as part of us, rather than as distinct and separate from us, we might start to understand the true nature of reality.

And Nature really is a phenomenal thing, isn't she? That things can grow, and evolve on their own, seemingly connected to an intelligence that exists somewhere in the ether.

Maybe Nature is God. Or Life is God.

Jesus also said, "I am the way, the truth and the life." Of interest, the word he uses for "life" is the Greek "zoe" which comes from the root "zau" which can also mean "to breathe."

Zen masters focus on the breath as a way of attaining mindfulness, and the yogic concept of *prana*, which surrounds and permeates all living things (aka "the Force"), is deeply connected with the breath. Maybe Jesus was speaking of an interconnectedness with the breath-of-life or lifeforce that exists in all living things. It is unfortunate that this bible verse is often used as a way of promoting a very limited version of Christianity as the only way to find God, as if God is something separate from our true Nature.

So maybe God *is* a cow, and God is also mom and dad. And maybe God is also a tree, and the wind, and a rock, and a building, and your neighbor, and the Force, and even you and me.

The Bhagavad Gita says, "those who have realized the Self see that same Self equally in a humble scholar, a cow, a dog or a dog-eater."[9] That Divine Self exists in all things and all things are interconnected by way of that inner divinity.

Part of the suffering we are experiencing as humans comes from the lack of connection we feel to our own inner divinity; the sense of separation we feel from our fellow humans and Nature; the so-called "mine and yours"—or "us and them"—mentalities that we cling to. It comes from judgment; which is both a precious gift and a great source of human suffering.

---

[9] Chapter 5:18

CHAPTER 3

Judgment

Judge not, and you will not be judged; condemn not, and you will not be condemned; forgive, and you will be forgiven.
~ Jesus to his disciples, <u>Luke</u> 6:37

...

Judge me by my size, do you? Hmm? Hmm. And well you should not. For my ally is the Force, and a powerful ally it is.
~ Yoda, <u>The Empire Strikes Back</u>

Is judgment really a bad thing?

Remember that entering the darkness is part of the classic human story we all share. We must go into the shadow; into the dark part of ourselves in order to find the treasure and emerge victorious. Exploring our human concepts of judgment and good and evil (next chapter) can be an important step on our individual journeys.

Personally, my quest led me to perceive that our brains are like judgment-combobulating-machines—constantly comparing objects and telling us things like, "this is better than that, and hers is better than yours, and people shouldn't do this but should do that, and this is right but that is wrong, and I would never do what he does or be like her, etc.

All. The. Time. It almost never stops. We are always judging everything.

In essence, it is our personal judgments that separate good from evil, and these concepts really only exist in our own minds.

This ability to judge is what separates us from animals. And we don't shit in the woods. (Well I'm not saying I haven't). But the most important difference is that generally, humans judge, animals don't. At least not in the same way we do or to the same extent. It is an evolutionary milestone, really, and it is the true meaning of the biblical story of Adam and Eve.

Whaaatt the bible again?

Indeed.

Remember that in the story, God warned Adam and Eve not to eat from the tree "of the knowledge of good and evil." Because if they did, they would "certainly die."[10]

Think about it. What is knowledge of good and evil but the ability to judge? Before we had knowledge of the difference between good things and bad things, or better things and worse things, we were at peace with whatever came our way. This is the way animals live. They do not lament their fate when things don't go their way like humans do.

But on a subtler level, do animals compare things like we do? We are always looking for the better thing - the better experience - because we have the ability judge the difference. I don't think we were always this way. I would guess that we once lived much more like animals, and were much more accepting of reality. We were probably also much more accepting of our fellow humans, realizing that the same "Force" that exists in us also exists in them.

The fact that we were maybe more ignorantly bliss at one point in human history doesn't make evolution a bad thing. Being able to judge is a precious gift: it makes us co-creators of our realities. And this book is full of judgments; my personal judgments. Being a good lawyer means being able to make judgments from different

---

[10] Genesis 2:17

perspectives and thereby anticipate arguments. It comes very naturally to me. Everyone is making judgments from their unique perspective all day long. That doesn't mean judgment is bad. But its best to judge with a level of detachment from being right and a genuine openness to other possibilities.

In the story, the serpent told Eve that she wouldn't die if she ate from the tree, but that her "eyes will be opened" and she would "be like God, knowing good and evil." After they ate it, Adam and Eve realized their own mortality and vulnerability, noticing for the first time that they were "naked."[11]

That is where we pick up with the human race as we know it. We have knowledge of good and evil, i.e., the ability to judge. This makes us like God because we have the ability to create our own reality with our judgments.

And we do create our reality with our ability to judge. We are able to choose things and experiences and discard others. But our frailty comes from our knowledge of bodily death, which makes us feel vulnerable and separate from Nature. When we lived like animals, we weren't concerned with death. We had no sense of separation from the oneness of life. The death of our physical body meant nothing to us because we had no

---

[11] Genesis 3:5-7

concept that it was separate from all of the rest of life. But now we fear death, which came with our ability to judge.

And this isn't really a bad thing, as the story may lead us to believe. I believe it is an important part of our evolutionary journey. Nature gave us the ability to judge, which gave us free will. Now we can choose to live with a sense of separation from the rest of the beings on Earth, or we can choose to come back to that sense of oneness that came naturally to us before we had the ability to choose.

Which brings up *another* Bible story. The story of the prodigal son. Remember that one? Here is the gist:

A man has two sons and decides to split up his fortune between them. One son—the prodigal son - skedaddles, engaging in all sorts of immoral acts and losing all of his money. After some time, he is starving with no food or shelter.

The older son is virtuous and stays with his father on the estate, helping him with farm duties and being an all-around-good-guy.

The prodigal son realizes that he what he did was wrong, and that now he is starving when even the hired men at his dad's farm have food to eat. He goes home and admits he was wrong and not worthy of being his father's son. He asks to be taken on as a hired man so that he may at least have some food to eat.

His dad is so overjoyed that his son has come back. He decides to throw a *huuge* party and kills the fatted calf, gives his son a bedazzled robe and fancy jewelry - the whole deal.

The older son is like, what gives? I've been here the whole time and worked hard for you, doing everything you asked me. Never have you celebrated me.

His father replied, "you and I are very close, and everything I have is yours. But it is right to celebrate. For he is your brother; and he was dead and has come back to life! He was lost and is found!"[12]

If we look at this story in context with the Adam and Eve story, the older brother is like the humans that existed prior to the knowledge of good and evil; he obeyed his father in every way. The prodigal son is more like Adam and Eve; he became aware of his ability to choose. Like I said before, I think this is part of our evolutionary journey. We can create and do wonderful things with our ability to judge and choose. The problem arises when the judgment gets extreme and we lose sight of our inherent oneness with all that is. Free will gives us the ability to choose not to judge, or better yet, to choose

---

[12] Luke 15:31-2

when to judge. Unity happens when we relinquish our ability to constantly judge and surrender to the inter-connectedness of life.

The parable of the prodigal son recognizes that there is something special about the path of going from a state of being lost (with a sense of separation from our divinity) to a state of being found (living in unity) - i.e. the way of the prodigal son. This is different from always living in a state of being found—i.e. the way of the older son. No doubt it would be awesome to start and stay in a state of unity, like the older son; but there is something particularly magical and celebration-worthy of reuniting after experiencing separation, like the prodigal son.

Maybe we chose to be here now on Earth because we want to become found after losing ourselves. Otherwise, maybe we would have been born in some other realm where we are born in a state of unity and never lose it. Maybe we are here because our souls love this dance of falling asleep and then waking up; of being lost and becoming found. The Hindus call it "Lila" or God's play.

In other words, maybe the Divine Nature inside of each of us delights in being obscured and then being revealed; it delights in falling asleep and then waking back up. This is our reward for victory in our personal hero's quest. This is the treasure that can be found when we confront the darkness and overcome evil.

CHAPTER 4

What is Good and Evil, Anyway?

Repel evil with what is better. Then will he, between whom and thee was hatred, become as it were thy friend and intimate.

~ The Qu'ran, Chapter 41, Verse 34

...

Your thoughts betray you, Father. I feel the good in you, the conflict.

~ Luke Skywalker, Return of the Jedi

We are all on a hero's journey, whether we realize it or not.

We humans are all on the journey of becoming found or experiencing oneness, though with many divergent paths.

Even humans that are doing things which many people would call "horrible" and "evil" are on a path. Call it a dark path, maybe, but it is a path nonetheless.

I believe people that engage in acts like violence, terrorism and even, more subtly, anger and aggression, do so only because they do not feel connected to the oneness of life. They feel separate from Nature and from other people. They resort to sorting and classifying humans according to their differences: Americans are better than Non-Americans, Christians are better than Non-Christians, natives are better than immigrants, etc.

If, as discussed in the last chapter, the difference between good and evil only came as a result of our ability to judge, was there really ever good or evil before humans were capable of perceiving same? And what is "evil," really? What is morality? Can there really be any set of rules that applies to all situations?

Even a mandate as simple as "thou shall not kill" certainly has exceptions. Across cultures we can see that what is acceptable to some is unacceptable to others. For instance, did you know in India it is offensive to eat with your left hand?

So maybe we can agree that left-hand-eating is less egregious a sin than killing. But what about the fact that we eat animals? In India, to eat a cow is highly offensive, as cows are considered sacred. In America, we wouldn't bat an eye over a cow or a pig, but talk about eating a dog or a horse and we flip out, though those things are acceptable in some cultures. The point is, one person's right can be another person's wrong quite easily, and there really aren't any universal morals that apply at all times in all situations.

We tend to demonize people who have done terrible things and treat them like monsters. We have a difficult time separating the person from the bad act. I recently saw a picture of Hitler holding hands with a young child, looking quite fatherly and sweet. The photograph blew the internet's mind. How can we reconcile our idea of Hitler as a monster with this photo showing him behaving kindly? Does. Not. Compute.

The truth is, Hitler was a person, not a monster. He committed horrible atrocities, but he was still a human and we are all connected to him through our shared humanity and existence on Earth. He truly believed what he was doing was right and that he was serving his country. He never saw himself as evil.

Did you know that Gandhi wrote letters to Hitler in 1939 and 1940 imploring him to stop the war? Gandhi wrote to Hitler:

Dear Friend,

That I address you as a friend is no formality. I own no foes. My business in life has been for the past 33 years to enlist the friendship of the whole of humanity by befriending mankind, irrespective of race, colour, or creed.

I hope you will have the time and desire to know how a good portion of humanity who [live] under the influence of that doctrine of universal friendship view your action. We have no doubt about your bravery or devotion to your fatherland, nor do we believe that you are the monster described by your opponents.

But your own writings and pronouncements and those of your friends and admirers leave no room for doubt that many of your acts are monstrous and unbecoming of human dignity, especially in the estimation of men like me who believe in universal friendliness.

Of note, Gandhi referred to Hitler as a "friend" and said that he does not believe that Hitler is a monster, but that many of *his actions* are monstrous. Gandhi, the great saint who espoused peace, separated the man from his acts and did not see Hitler as inherently evil.

We love to create these black and white situations in our mind about who is good and who is evil, but the truth is that we are all a little of both. Even Gandhi had his human faults. We project all of our bad qualities - those qualities we suppress and refuse to come to terms with in ourselves - onto our enemies. And let's face it, some of our enemies subjectively deserve it. There are people who spew hatred and promote violence, and most of us would agree that those things are bad.

However, hating the haters doesn't solve the problem. But we love to hate the haters, don't we? It makes us feel righteous. It is bad for Neo-Nazis or White Supremacists, for example, to spew hatred but it is okay to hate them for doing it, right?

But to hate anyone, even people that might subjectively or even objectively deserve it, is to feed the darkness monster. It only creates more hate. The real wisdom—the real compassion—comes from seeing people like Hitler as human. He is a human who did horrible things based on some messed up beliefs and judgments. Looking at him and other haters in that way begs the question: in what way, on a smaller scale, do I engage in limiting beliefs and judgments? In what ways do I separate myself from other humans with my judgments about how we are different, rather than recognizing that there is an essential part of us that is shared?

That is, deep down, we are all made of the same stuff. Maybe we think of it as empty space, air, prana, lifeforce, The Force, ether, God-stuff, Nature, or Consciousness. The truth is, if I was born where you were born, at the time you were born, to your parents, with your genes, with your karmas and life circumstances, and grew up with exactly your history, *I would be you.*

We are all the product of our own personal circumstances; of our unique experience of nature and nurture. We like to think we are different from people like Hitler. We like to think thoughts like, "I would *never* do that," making ourselves feel better.

But the truth is I would be Hitler if my life was his life.

That is, in my experience, our material bodies are more like a shell that our divine essence plugs into. It is as if God said, "I want to experience reality as *Kelli*" and, boom, there you go: I was born on Earth.

You're welcome.

And then God said, I want to experience reality as a person born here, with these difficulties, and these personality traits, and these life events, and these parents, and boom, there you go, *You* were born. Or, boom, your "enemy" was born. At our essence, we are all the same.

Explore that. Don't take my word for it. Leave space for the possibility that it's true and see what happens.

Realizing that those we dislike are our mirrors is not a new concept in the spiritual quest. It is part of exploring our "shadow side." It is a practice of looking at the people and situations that really bother us and realizing that the source of those emotions comes from inside— the people and situations act as triggers, but are not the source of the emotion.

This can be grouped under the yogic practice of *pratyahara*; one of the eight limbs of Patanjali's Ashtanga Yoga, that we will discuss in more detail later on. In short, it is a withdrawal of the senses and feelings inward to their source, rather than the constant outward projection that most of us are used too. It starts with the recognition that we are all in this together; all humans are our brothers and sisters.

The fact that deep down, everyone is the same doesn't mean we shouldn't create boundaries, use caution, or otherwise protect ourselves from those who would act in unkind ways. There is a difference between cutting someone out of your life and cutting them out of your heart.

At the time of this writing, Donald Trump is the president of the United States. He inspires a lot of haters. He also has a lot of supporters, who connect with his passion and frankness in speaking his mind.

Truth be told, he has, at times, said racist and sexist things and even encouraged violence. He condones the building of walls (literally and figuratively)[13] and clearly feels a sense of separation from lots of other humans. But to engage with him at that level makes no sense. To come at him and those that support him with hatred only fuels the fire and promotes the story of "us" versus "them." Furthermore, it alienates members of our own inner circles and families, the people we love.

So how to act? How to keep an open heart? We have to learn to separate the person from their beliefs. We can feel love and kindness toward the person, even though we disagree with their beliefs and actions. We can find common ground and stay above the fray. We cannot devolve into violence or fighting at the level of the problem. We must take the high road, and maintain dignity and respect for the individual person - even while disagreeing with that person—and work toward a world of oneness, not separation. Keeping an open

---

[13] Remember Pope Francis said to build walls and not bridges is unchristian, and was speaking figuratively about walls in our hearts and minds. <http://www.cnn.com/2016/02/18/politics/pope-francis-trump-christian-wall/index.html>

heart is the key; and realizing that people are not the same as their arguments and beliefs.

Our villains exist because our personal stories require that they exist. Innately, we recognize that we are on a hero's quest and that we must face darkness before realizing victory. We project this darkness onto our perceived villains. But do the villains themselves ever believe that they are villains? Did Hitler believe he was a villain? Does Donald Trump or do his supporters agree with people who call him a villain and compare him to Hitler? Of course not. They have an entirely different and equally valid perception.

Instead, we must elevate the story. We must recognize our shared humanity with our enemies. Instead of demonizing those we disagree with, let's think of them like you think of your Great Aunt Lily who says crazy political and/or racist stuff every Thanksgiving: well-meaning but misguided, at least from our point of view. (Because from her also-subjectively-correct point of view, we are the misguided ones). We must recognize that deep down, we are all the same.

But how can we do that? I certainly would not ask you to start believing in my concept of God or sameness any more than I would ask you to believe in any other concept of God, or anything else for that matter. I believe that divinity is something that must be experienced, not believed. Faith based on blind belief is a double-edged sword that has gotten us humans into a lot of trouble.

So how about that quest we've been talking about? You like adventure don't you? A personal quest of self-discovery is the only tried-and-true way to really experience what divinity means for you. And once you have that experience, no one can take it away from you; and you will no longer need to rely on faith or belief.

II. Practice

tapah svadhyaya Isvara pranidhanani kriya yoga

"purification (tapas), self-study (svadhyaya), and devotion to one's personal concept of divinity (Ishvara pranidhanani) are the practical means for attaining higher consciousness"

~ Sutra II-1, The Yoga Sutras of Patanjali

CHAPTER 5

The Quest

If you are brave enough to leave behind everything familiar and comforting (which can be anything from your house to your bitter old resentments) and set out on a truth-seeking journey (either externally or internally), and if you are truly willing to regard everything that happens to you on that journey as a clue, and if you accept everyone you meet along the way as a teacher, and if you are prepared—most of all—to face (and forgive) some very difficult realities about yourself... then truth will not be withheld from you.
~ Elizabeth Gilbert, <u>Eat, Pray, Love</u>

...

The belonging you seek is not behind you... it is ahead. I am no Jedi, but I know the Force. It moves through and

surrounds every living thing. Close your eyes... Feel it...
The light... it's always been there. It will guide you.

~ Maz Kanata, <u>Star Wars: The Force Awakens</u>

My personal quest for truth led me to India.

However, the location of the quest is irrelevant. It is really an inner journey that must be undertaken.

It is a conscious decision that one undertakes to treat life as a quest; to notice synchronicities and coincidences, and to be open to everything that comes along the way. You don't need to go to India or to an ashram or find a cave to meditate in. It happens right when you decide it happens, while you work at your seemingly mundane job, and go about your apparently ordinary existence.

All that really has to be done to start on the quest is to set the intention to do so. Looking back often at circumstances and events that occur in our day-to-day lives with an eye for perceiving deeper meaning is helpful too.

One of the most pivotal moments in my personal inner adventure occurred about a month after arriving home from a trip to Mysore in 2014. I was engaged in mundane tasks for sure—dealing with City ordinances and red tape in order to sell Daniel's house - an investment property we had all planned to work on and flip together before he died and plans changed.

I had a dream about Daniel while I was in India, where he sat me down and told me that I needed to take a look back at his death. I wasn't sure what he meant at the time, but I've come to realize that I hadn't been exactly dealing with my grief head-on. It had been subtle—like avoiding places and things that made me think of him.

We had been trying to sell his house in Debary, a small town in Central Florida near where I grew up for a long time. As the sale was about to close, we got word from the City that there was a lien on the property for over $47,000—almost double the sale price of $25k—due to a broken fence section on the property.

Turns out the City had been sending notices directly to Daniel, who had been gone for over 4 years at the time, and the $50-a-day fines had amassed to a whopping $47k—making the sale of the house impossible.

In order to get the fines reduced or waived, my mom was told she would have to bring the issue before the City at the upcoming quarterly meeting at City Hall.

So I headed up to City Hall in Debary, Florida, on a crisp night in January, only to see hundreds of people wearing red shirts swarming the City Hall building. News crews and police officers were also present.

That's because the agenda for the evening was focused on the development of a new Walmart—an issue hotly contested and vehemently opposed by the local townsfolk—and tons of people showed up to rally against the proposed development.

I walked into the meeting and got there early enough to grab a seat near the front. (Also, I was dressed as Lawyer-Kelli and you'd be surprised at how easy it is for her to get a seat at the front of any meeting).

By the time the meeting started, all seats were filled and a couple hundred people were standing along the walls in the back—probably over 1000 people total. The only issue on the agenda was Walmart-gate, but a nice lady in the seat next to me told me I could talk about my issue during the open public forum prior to the agenda discussion. I had to fill out a form to speak which I handed directly to the *actual mayor*, who was standing at the podium. Also present were the City Manager, the City Attorney, and all members of the City Council.

The meeting started with a prayer (is that normal?) and then the floor opened for non-agenda items. We would each get three minutes to speak about our issues. There was a giant clock on the mayor's podium counting down our time. It felt surreal—like a game show. The first non-agenda speaker was called up. He gave an enthusiastic and erratic speech during which the microphone died about 30 seconds in, requiring him to start over and regain his original enthusiasm.

Then I was called up. No problems with the mic this time. I gave my passionate plea about my brother's house; about how the lien against the property was prohibiting the sale and that all that my poor mom and I wanted was "closure" so that we could move forward from Daniel's death. I closed by explaining how we wanted to get the new owners in so that they can "start making the property an asset to the neighborhood." (I had rehearsed it many times). When I was done, I had I talked about his death to a huge group of people.

As I gave my impassioned speech, the mayor, City Manager and all council members nodded in solidarity with me and slow-clapped. I could feel all attention in the room on me and it was as though every single person in the crowd felt my pain. After I stepped down, the City Manager asked me for the address of the property so that he could personally look into it for me.

As I was handing him the address, a woman swiftly approached me with a fixed gaze. I looked behind me and forward again. Was she looking for someone else? No, she was clearly coming to talk directly to me.

She said that I was probably looking for the special magistrate hearing in the building just behind this one.

I was in the wrong fucking place.

I had just given a speech in front of probably over a thousand people, the news media, the police, the mayor, and the entire city council. And I wasn't even at the right meeting.

The City Manager kindly showed me the back-door-super-secret-shortcut-way to get to *my* meeting, by walking through the back City Hall corridor. I ran over there as fast as I could and scooted into a seat just as they were calling our case. I gave the same impassioned plea in front of the special magistrate, the code enforcement clerk, and four audience members—a total of six people. The special magistrate agreed to waive the fines and lien. Case closed.

Welp, Daniel, I suppose that's one way to face my stuff head on.

It was exhilarating and fun. I felt like Leslie Knope from Parks and Recreation. And it felt like Daniel had orchestrated the whole thing and was laughing his ass off backstage. I could picture it in vivid clarity. Even thinking about it now makes my eyes well up; I see and hear his laugh in my head just as clearly.

My quest for truth had led me into a funny mini-climax in the drama of my life. I wanted to overcome my grief, and I was open to the path my life would take to get me there. Most importantly, I trusted that life was working for me and I went with the flow.

Since that day, my life shifted dramatically. I felt a renewed since of purpose and focus. I didn't realize the ways that my unattended-to grief had been holding me back. I believe that many of us are walking around with unattended-to emotions. We carry them in our backs, necks, and shoulders and I can see "the weight of the world" on many people I encounter.

As you embark on your own personal quest, I recommend being open to the feelings and beliefs that may be holding you back. Undertake practices that help to burn up some of that old stuff—like yoga, meditation, walks in nature, prayer, etc. The beauty of this path is that there is no one right way. It is really the intention that matters most, along with the passion and determination to stay with it until the Truth is revealed. As said by Swami Vivekananda, a Hindu Saint:

> As different streams having their sources in different places all mingle their waters in the sea, so, Oh Lord, the different paths which men take through different tendencies various though they appear, crooked or straight, all lead to Thee.

No two quests will look the same, and there is no "one size fits all" approach or moral framework that will work for everyone. The point is to just do it. And you don't have to force yourself to change in order to begin. You start where you are, with all of your perceived faults and vices.

No two quests will look the same, and there is no "one size fits all" approach or moral framework that will work for everyone. The point is to just do it. And you don't have to force yourself to change in order to begin. You start where you are, with all of your perceived faults and vices.

CHAPTER 6

Do I Have to Quit Drinkin'/Smokin'/ Lovin'?

Bowling Priest: You see, bowling for money... that's my only vice.
Cocktail Waitress: Here's your drink.
Bowling Priest: Thanks sugar.
[takes double bourbon on the rocks and pats waitress' behind]
Bowling Priest: Okay, two vices.
Ernie McCracken: That's still very good.

~ Kingpin

...

You like me because I'm a scoundrel. There aren't enough scoundrels in your life.

~ Han Solo, Empire Strikes Back

The beauty about our quest is that we don't have to change anything to get started.

The quest starts right where we are right now, with all of our supposed unhealthy habits and attitudes. The key is to be open to change, while not forcing it upon ourselves.

One of my favorite all-time yogis is Paramahansa Yogananda, author of "Autobiography of a Yogi." He died in 1952, but his words have lived on, influencing many people, including Steve Jobs. In fact, Steve Jobs was said to have made sure copies of Yogananda's book were given out to attendees at his memorial service as his last gift to friends and family.

There is a story about Yogananda and a seeker who asked the great yogi if he would have to give up his smoking, drinking, and lovin' in order to traverse the spiritual path. Yogananda famously replied that no, he would not have to give up those things. He further stated, "But I can't promise that the desire for those things won't leave you."

And that is the way it goes on the spiritual path, at least in my experience. I've tried to give up what I perceived as unhealthy habits or beliefs by shear force, with limited success. Remember, this Nature/God/Lifeforce/The Force/Essence is nonjudgmental. Our concepts of good and bad are more human than divine.

I mentioned before that Grandma Teddy would teach me and Daniel (and our cousins) lessons using stories about Rotten Minerva getting into trouble and learning from her mistakes.

And I did grow up to be pretty rotten, or naughty, from a certain point of view. At least, I don't feel like your typical "holy Yogi." I like to drink fine wines and hoppy bear, indulge in foodie grub, and play poker and cuss, among other things.

And yet, I feel driven by a divine connection and, above all, I feel that I must be true to that connection. In other words, if I feel called to take a certain action in my heart, I heed that advice. I feel that being authentic to that little voice of my highest self inside is important above all else.

I find that the more I trust it, the more I realize that it steers me in the right direction. When I'm truly listening to it, my life seems to unfold with magical ease.

I think it's okay to be a little "rotten." I don't think it's completely possible to deny our materiality by denying our enjoyment of life. Jesus said to be in this world, not of it.[14] We can't deny that we are here on Earth and that we embody a physical, human form. We have to eat, sleep and defecate. We cannot completely deny our humanity.

And we can't deny our spirituality. It will keep knocking on our door in the form of our life circumstances until we wake up to the reality of it. We must strike a balance between living a physical and spiritual existence. The world needs us to do this. We need human beings that exist in this world and that embody spirituality. We need doctors, lawyers, politicians, teachers, bus drivers, therapists, hair dressers, waiters, bartenders, clerks, flight attendants, musicians, artists and others, that are in this world and not of it.

The spiritual quest doesn't judge and divinity can be experienced anytime, anywhere. As it turns out, I've had divine experiences at the hand of one of my favorite vices—marijuana. How 'bout another story?

During my second trip to Mysore, I was having trouble finding weed. Marijuana has been a form of self-medication for me; helping me deal with my anxiety

---

[14] Paraphrased from John 17:6-19

and muscle pain, along with making me feel more connected to the Divine.

As a side-note, I feel I should take this opportunity to shout out some of the positive traits of this amazing herb. Daniel and my Dad used it during their cancer treatments to alleviate side effects, and studies have shown that it actually can treat cancer by shrinking cancer cells and encouraging healthy cell growth.[15] And from a holistic, herbalist perspective, Cannabis can be considered an adaptogen, meaning that it offers a broad spectrum of positive effects, depending on the needs of the specific individual taking it. Crazy that this wonderful herb is still so vilified.

Times, they are a changing, and the decriminalization and legalization of medical marijuana is happening slowly but surely. And I'm all for it.

Back to my India-marijuana-story: I decided it was time to take matters into my own hands. I knew there was plenty of weed around and that it was easy enough to get based on my prior trip to Mysore. But this time, I

---

15 Guzman, M., "Cannabinoids: potential anticancer agents" Nature Reviews Cancer 3, 745-755 (October 2003); Cridge, B and Rosengren, R., "Critial Appraisal of the potential use of cannabinoids in cancer management" Cancer Management and Research, 2013:5, 301-313 (August 29, 2013); Hermanson, D. and Marnett, L., "Cannabinoids, endocannabinoids, and cancer" Cancer and Metastasis Reviews, 30:3, 599-612 (December 2011).

was having difficulty finding any connections. I thought about Daniel, and how whenever we traveled together he had such an easy time finding herb.

One time he even was able to buy weed while we strolled with our parents through a super-touristy-cruise-ship-port. My parents had no clue. (Though my mom did ask rhetorically, "what is ganja?" as if having head, the word said wistfully on the breeze, but still having no idea that Daniel was buying said ganja at that exact moment). Impressive. Most impressive. He was.

I decided to do what I thought he would have done—go to a city-center-market-type-place and ask the "right type" of person.

Channeling Daniel, I headed down to the rickshaw stand where there are normally 10-20 rickshaws and drivers to choose from. I was deep in thoughtful planning the whole walk there, thinking things like, "I have to find the right rickshaw driver. One that doesn't seem too shady or too not-shady-enough..."

When I got to the rickshaw stand, unfortunately, there was only *one* rickshaw driver, for like the first time ever. I guess this one will have to do, I thought.

Om, Daniel, Om.

I got in the rickshaw and told him to take me to the market. After starting in that direction, he asked, "what are you going to buy?" I hesitated for a moment, and then decided just to lay it out there: "I really want to get some marijuana."

He paused, and I instantly regretted my decision. Then he said slowly, "you don't want to go to the market for marijuana. It is cut with incense and is no good. I'll take you to a special shop in town."

Awesome, ok, let's do it.

After a few more minutes of driving he asked me, "Do you want any oils or incense?" I thought, "what the eff? Didn't we just discuss what I want?" I replied more politely than my judgy-brain-voice wanted me to respond: "No, I really just want marijuana."

He laughed.

We got to the shop and it was a little dark and dank. I was led to the back of the shop where I was told to duck because the doorway was low. I thought, "Why is this guy telling me to duck, I can take care of myself!"

I was a little on edge and in full internal judgment mode. I was slightly concerned for my safety, but there really was no reason to be. We were in the middle of a busy district and I truly felt Daniel with me. Whenever I thought of him, my fear dissipated.

I was introduced to the shopkeeper, Shahib who had welcoming eyes and an extremely friendly demeanor. He reminded me of Deepak Chopra and I felt at ease in his presence. He offered me chai tea and incense and oils.

I looked at my rickshaw driver with side-eye like, "didn't you give him my message?"

I refused his offer and said, "I really just want marijuana." Shahib laughed heartily and told me it would take about ten minutes for it arrive and that while we wait, I should enjoy some chai and try his oils. (By the way, it seems like everything in India takes about 10 minutes—the locals are fond of responding, "just now coming" to questions like, "where is the shopkeeper?" "when will the food arrive?" "what time is the train?" etc.)

Alright, I guess I'm down.

I relaxed and tried the tea and oils. The tea was great and his oils were amazing. Sandalwood, frankincense, tulsi, and lemongrass and many, many more. Better than any I had ever tried before. We chatted for much more than ten minutes (Indian culture *really* doesn't follow the same concept of time we follow in the West). I had found a new life-long friend. I still visit Shahib every time I go to India (mostly for the oils, ahem), and I have had dinner at his house with his family.

After some time, I got my "stuff" and headed out. As I was walking out, I whacked my head really hard on the doorway I was instructed to watch out for on my way in.

I got back in the rickshaw with Sai, the driver, feeling very light and happy that my herb-quest had went so well. Sai looked up at me in the rearview mirror as we departed, smiling, and said, "God is good."

I smiled inside and out, really feeling the truth of what he said. I replied, yes, "God is good." Then, he pointed to a picture of Jesus on the front of his rickshaw.

I laughed and thought, well what do you know? Jesus was with us the whole time. But as my eyes moved from the picture of Jesus toward the center of his windshield my jaw dropped. Written in broad letters across the front was the name, "Daniel."

What the wha..? Are you kidding me? What are the chances? I laugh-cried maniacally from the backseat. His rickshaw seriously had my brother's name written on it in huge letters.

Sai became my permanent rickshaw driver, and I still use his mad driving skills for all my travels while I'm in Mysore. He too, became a close friend, and I've been to his house and met his family.

I later learned that his brother's son—Sai's nephew— is named Daniel, and that is why he put that name on the front of his rickshaw. It is common to see rickshaws covered with names and pictures of deities and family members. Still, I'm fairly certain Sai's is the only one in all of India that says, "Daniel" (not a common name in India). To me, it was a real-life miracle; confirmation that Daniel was with me and I was on the right path.

And this all happened because I needed a weed fix? Sort of.

Maybe it happened because I was destined to connect with Sai and Shabib. Or maybe it happened because I was open to going with the flow in spite of some mental judgments to the contrary. Nature doesn't judge and neither should I.

Divine experiences can come to us at any time. They can even come out of seemingly "negative" things. The key is remaining open and in the present moment even when our brains want us to judge and close up. Judgments are like cataracts; the block us from our perceiving all of the possibilities available to us at any moment; and instead limit us to our common reactions.

As I've continued on the spiritual path, I've found that, as Yogananda predicted, my desire for harmful things has dwindled, and I am naturally drawn to things that are healthy for my mind and body. Not because anything is "bad," but because I am more open to hearing what my body and my heart truly want.

What is harmful to me might be great for you and vice-versa. The point is that if we truly wish to live healthier lives with less reliance on negative vices and

hurtful emotions and judgments, we should devote ourselves to the spiritual quest.

That is the real yoga. With that devotion to the quest,
often a healthier existence comes naturally, without the
struggle and judgments that come with forcing yourself
to do something you aren't ready to do.

CHAPTER 7

The Real Yoga

Fill your mind with me; love me; serve me; worship me always. Seeking me in your heart, you will at last be united with me.

~ The Bhagavad Gita

...

I'm one with the Force. The Force is with me.

~ Chirrut Imwe, Star Wars: Rogue One

The real yoga isn't practiced in a gym or yoga studio, and doesn't even necessarily involve your physical body. Wait. Let's back up. What *is* yoga?

The Yoga Sutras say, *yoga citta vritti nirodha*, "yoga is the state where the fluctuating waves of thought are calm."

Thus, yoga is a state of being.

It is interesting that Patanjali uses the Sanskrit word "*nirodha*" to represent the "calming of thought" because that word literally translates to "without Rudra," who is the god of storms.

So the state of *being in yoga* occurs when the *storms* of the mind are calmed. That is a little different than a state of no thought, as it is often inaccurately described. Instead, it is a state of calm thought.

In addition, the word yoga comes from the same root as the word "yoke" and can mean "to join together" or "union," as in, "yoga is the joining together of mind, body, and spirit."

But the term "yoga" is also used colloquially to describe the practices that help bring us into that state of calmness of mind or union.

In the Yoga Sutras, Patanjali describes the eight limbs of yoga practice: *yama, niyama, asana, pranayama, pratyahara, dharana, dhyana, samadhi*. Briefly, the *yamas* and *niyamas* are moral and ethical observances and practices (including *tapas* and *svadhyaya*) [16]; *asana* refers to the physical postures; *pranayama* is yogic breathing practices; *pratyahara* is sense withdrawal; *dharana* is concentration; *dhyana* is meditation; and *samadhi* is supreme bliss or super consciousness.

It is interesting that in the West, we are predominantly exposed to yoga *asana*, and many people associate "yoga" with just the physical exercise of yoga postures. In fact, *asana* is only one of eight limbs of yoga, and represents only a small subset of the breadth of yoga practices available. *Asana*, while a beneficial and important yogic practice, is arguably not the most efficient or practical way to get to the state of being in "yoga."

In fact, the teacher[17] of one of the most famous yoga *asana* teachers of modern history explained that the real yoga is the devotional practice of constantly directing one's mind toward the Supreme Self. He advocated a

---

[16] *Tapas* are physical and metaphysical purification practices, *svadhyaya* is self-study. Both are useful tools that will be mentioned again in later chapters.

[17] Shri K. Pattabhi Jois was referred to as "Guruji" by his students, and is credited with popularizing a style of *asana* which is still taught in Mysore, Karnataka, India by his daughter, Saraswathi, and grandson, Sharath. In fact, to practice this style of *asana* with Guruji's family is one of the reasons I traveled to Mysore. I never personally practiced with Guruji; he died right before I started practicing yoga *asana*.

constant practice of yoga in his book, "The Yoga Mala," but was not referring to physical postures, which he had stopped practicing many years earlier:

> *Therefore, if the mind is to be steadied and brought to concentration, it must contemplate the Supreme Self at all times. In other words, whether working, sleeping, eating, playing, or even enjoying intercourse with one's wife—that is, during the three states of experience namely waking, dreaming, and deep sleep, and in all objects—one should think of the Supreme Self at all times.*

This *Ishvara pranidhana* practice of constantly remembering the Divine or Supreme Self is also known as *bhakti* yoga, or the yoga of devotion, as discussed earlier.

If the end goal is union, or the calming of the storms of the mind through the realization of oneness, then the practice of devotion (i.e. *bhakti* Yoga or *Ishvara pranidhana*) is probably the simplest way to reach that goal.

In the Yoga Sutras, while Patanjali sets forth many means and practices, he also suggests that devotion is the simplest way that one can attain the state of yoga without all the pomp and circumstance stating, "perfected bliss can be obtained through devotion."[18]

The Bhagavad Gita likewise states that path of devotion is the easier path for "embodied beings," like us humans, who naturally want to connect with divinity as something "other" or outside of ourselves.[19]

What does it mean to practice devotion? Like everything, it can mean different things depending on your perspective. The Bhagavad Gita and the Yoga Sutras teach that oneness can be achieved through duality when we practice devotion to our personal concept of divinity.

To me, devotion is a way of utilizing to our spiritual advantage our natural human tendency toward duality.

In other words, if the natural tendency of our constantly-judging-minds is to separate the world into opposites, then we can use that tendency to perceive divinity in everything. First, it is perceived as separate from ourselves: there is me and there is God. But the more we witness it, the more it merges into oneness with our own being. The practice of devotion is a constant remembering of the divine, which at first is

---

[18] Sutra II, 45.
[19] Bhagavad Gita, Chapter 12, verse 5.

perceived as something "other" than ourselves, but eventually becomes one with us.

The practice of devotion feels natural to people like me with strong emotions; and strong emotions need not be avoided. Instead, they are used as a means of getting closer and closer to our highest Self.

Swami Vivekananda described it this way in "Bhakti yoga: The Yoga of Love and Devotion: "The Bhakta [bhakti practitioner] has not to suppress any single one of his emotions, he only strives to intensify them and direct them to God."

Therefore, the "real yoga" isn't about stretching and bending our bodies; it is the constant practice of redirecting our thoughts and emotions toward the divine until we become one with it. In that state of yoga, we experience bliss, which transcends happiness and duality. Whoa.

But this really isn't a book about yoga. Really.

I am a yogi so my quest involves yoga. But Yoga is just a framework that we can connect with for both realizing and describing the Divine. In the next chapter, I'll describe another useful framework. But for you, you might find a different framework makes more sense. You don't have to be a yogi to undertake your quest or to transcend duality and experience bliss. Though yoga, especially the yoga of devotion, is one tried-and-true means of getting there.

Everyone's quest is different. Don't let the words I use to describe my path turn you off from yours. The important thing is to undertake to walk your path with commitment and passion. I believe it is the most important thing you will ever do; humankind urgently needs heroes to launch their quests and recover their hidden treasures of the soul.

CHAPTER 8

Film Appreciation

Your vision will become clear only when you can look into your own heart. Who looks outside, dreams; who looks inside, awakes.

~ Carl Jung

...

In my experience, there is no such thing as luck.

~ Ben Kenobi, <u>Star Wars</u>

Life is like the Truman Show.

Well, maybe we aren't literally living in a television show or movie, but shifting our perception into a film appreciation mentality can hasten awakening.

And the theory that life is like a movie or game isn't all that crazy.

Elon Musk says we are living in computer simulation. (And he is pretty smart, right? Perhaps a super genius, even). Actually, he says the chances are a billion to one that we *are not* living in a computer simulation.

His theory goes something like this: technology has advanced exponentially in the last 40 years. Forty years ago, we were playing monochrome video games like "Pong" and they seemed awesome. Now, video games are hyper-realistic and there are even 3-D virtual reality simulation-type games available.

So, based on the advances in technology that have occurred in the last 40 years alone, it seems highly likely that in 40 or 50—or even 100 or 200—years from now, computer games will be indistinguishable from our "base" reality.

And from a yogic perspective, that might already be an accurate way to describe this "unreal" reality.

It's almost like our highest, deepest Selves are playing a game. The yogis call it *Lila*, or "God's play." In it, we are in the movie, the game, or the projected "reality." And in it, the goal is to become conscious that we are in a game, and not in what Elon musk would call a "base" reality.

Once we become conscious of that, we can align with our highest Selves. We aren't capable of understanding all the inter-workings of the game with our puny human minds; but we can get direction from that part of us that is capable.

In other words, at our essence or highest Self, we are capable of seeing the entire game and all its inner workings all the time. So we know the best choice to take at any given moment.

Once we realize that, perhaps we have the choice upon our next death to decide whether we want to stay in the "base" reality of unity rather than manifesting again into this transitory world of separation.[20]

If this is true, how can we connect with and learn from that base reality right now? What tools can we use on the quest to help us realize our highest Selves, aka the programmers of the game, aka the directors of our movie?

Actually, I find the movie metaphor particularly useful. When we watch a movie with an eye toward film appreciation, we look at everything that happens as a choice made by the director to further the story. From

---

[20] The Bhagavad Gita says, "when people die who know the truth of the Self, instead of taking another birth, they obtain oneness with me [God]." Chapter 5:18.

the numbers written above a door in the frame, to the colors of the clothes worn by the actors, to the sound-track—everything conveys an intended meaning by the storyteller.

Carl Jung, the famed psychiatrist, tells a story of movie-like synchronicity.[21] He was treating a patient who was describing a dream in which she was given a golden scarab beetle. As Jung listened to his patient, he heard a tapping on the window behind him. He turned around, opened the window, and caught a real-life scar-ab beetle that was making the noise. Her dream symbol had appeared in real life. At that moment, Jung realized that dream-like symbolism can seep into our waking reality.

Maybe reality is more like a dream than we realize. I believe it is. That is why I often say I am "living the dream" when someone asks me how I am doing. By that I mean, life is a dream and the point is to *live it* - consciously, with awareness.

Several years ago, I was in a depression, walking around my favorite lake and wondering to myself whether God was really listening and whether things

---

[21] <u>Synchronicity: An Acasual Principle</u> (1952); The Collected Works of C.G. Jung.

really are all connected or if life is really just a shitty mess of suffering before death.

I had the thought, "Hello, God, are you even there?"

At that moment, I walked by a woman who was deeply focused on the cell phone call she was in the process of making. She looked up from her phone at the precise second I passed by with my God-question and spoke directly right into my eyes as if in response to my silent thought:

"Hi, Kelli."

The coincidence was too startling not to notice. I asked God if she was listening and she said, "Hi Kelli" back to me, instantaneously.

Sure it could just be a meaningless happenstance, but it is just as possible that the director of my personal movie doesn't work that way: maybe everything in my movie was put there to further my personal story.

Great directors do that. Like in the Matrix, there are so many important details happening all around the characters all of the time. For example, Trinity whose name is of course symbolic for the holy trinity and the number 3, lives in apartment number 303; and Neo, whose name is an anagram for "one"—lives in apartment number 101.

Is that a meaningless coincidence or was that an intentional choice by the director?

We have to assume everything in a movie is there for a reason; that every single detail is a conscious choice from the movie director.

What if our life were like that?

Treating life like a movie by looking for coincidences, metaphors and symbols is another way of listening to your heart and following your quest. Our hearts are persistent. They will continue to lead us to on our divine path.

We can begin to do this just by noticing what happens each day and, particularly, what signs and symbols seem to repeat themselves.

For example, I might notice a turtle on my path during a walk. Later, I might pass by a billboard with a picture of a turtle on it that catches my attention. Maybe after that, my son coincidentally brings home a toy turtle from school. That's three turtles in one day and worth noticing. I might look up turtle symbolism and find out that turtles are symbolic of the ability to stay grounded amidst chaos and realize how deeply that applies to my life at this moment.

It's actually pretty easy and fun to begin noticing the signs all around us in our own personal, life-movie-quests. And what are the best types of movies? To me, they are the ones that surprise me; the ones where I could not see the ending coming. I hate when I can predict an outcome.

Yet in real life, if I can't figure out *right now* how my desired result will manifest, I tend to get negative and give up hope. Invoking the movie metaphor helps me in these situations. I think of another time in my past where I got an unexpected, unpredictable, happy-surprise outcome. (Like when I unexpectedly won my red light camera case and became kinda-sorta-locally-famous). Those types of surprises could not be planned even if we wanted to, and why would we want to?

In my experience, my highest Self is a great director—one that I wouldn't want to second guess. And even though I might not be able to see how it will all work out right now on my quest, I remember that it is very possible I'll be surprised. Doing so opens up space for possibilities.

III. Magic

Pratibhat va sarvam

"or all knowledge can be given through a flash of intuitive illumination"

~ Sutra III, 34, <u>Yoga Sutras of Patanjali</u>

CHAPTER 9

Leaving Space for Possibilities

Why do you stay in prison when the door is so wide open?

~ Rumi

...

So you're telling me there's a chance!

~ Lloyd Christmas, <u>Dumb and Dumber</u>

...

Never tell me the odds.

~ Han Solo, <u>The Empire Strikes Back</u>

Leaving space for possibilities is a way of staying open while remaining a healthy skeptic.

It is a way of catching yourself when your brain thinks things like, "I'll never be able to travel like I want to," or, "I'll never have a career doing what I love when I have bills to pay."

Instead of believing the thoughts, leaving space for possibilities is as simple as realizing that those thoughts *might* not be true.

I mean, they might true, but they also might not be... right?

That is, maybe it is at least possible that I could do the thing my thoughts say I can't do, even if the odds are low.

I mean, how low can they really be? One in ten? One in hundred? One in a million?

At least there is a chance; and that is all that really matters: realizing that it really isn't a "never" ... maybe it is just a really, really, low chance.

Poker is an apt metaphor for life and learning how to leave space for possibilities in life.

Poker is about maximizing odds, taking advantage of favorable position and circumstances, and thinking a step or two ahead. I love poker. It's my only vice.

(Well, maybe two or three vices ... (*cough*)).

Funny enough, good ol' Grandma Teddy (of Rotten Minerva fame) taught me how to play poker. I love the math of it, the people reading, the energy swings, the extreme focus it requires, and the luck, superstitions and synchronicities.

And, like I said, poker involves odds and maximizing odds in favorable situations.

Life is like that too. There is a lot we can't control; but we can maximize our odds by going with the flow and taking advantage of favorable circumstances.

Poker is also about letting go and moving on when things don't go our way; even when the odds were really, really stacked in our favor and we believed the win was guaranteed. Things can go wrong, and that is poker. That is also life.

In poker, there can also be miraculous wins, against all odds.

There is always a chance.

And in my experience, just realizing that there is a chance is enough to really open up a whole new world of possibilities in life.

In other words, it is good to take action in life based on logic and reason, but it is also good to leave space for the possibility that unexpected and happy surprises and miracles can and do happen. If we close ourselves off to those possibilities mentally—and out loud with our spoken words—then we literally close those types of possibilities from our lives. Our beliefs create our perceptions, and we are less able to perceive all of the choices that are available to us at any given moment if those choices are outside of the realm of our beliefs.

This may sound a little like "The Secret" and other self-help-manifesting-type lingo. I guess it is a little, but I do not wholly subscribe to the positive-thinking-necessarily-creates-a-positive-reality-and-vice-versa line of thinking.

It is true that thinking positive or thinking negative can shape our perceptions of reality. But just because something good or bad happens in our lives does not mean that it was the pure consequence of negative or positive thinking. There are a multitude of other factors involved, many of which are completely out of our control.

Most interestingly, the desire for positive experience is, itself a negative experience and the acceptance of a negative experience is, itself a positive experience. Alan Watts called this "the backwards law," and used the following metaphor: "When you try to stay on the surface of the water you sink; but when you try to sink you float."

That is, placing undue emphasis on positive experiences can actually create a negative experience; while surrendering to and accepting negative experiences in our lives can be a positive experience.

Life is both good and bad and we cannot entirely get rid of one or other because the two cannot exist without each other. There cannot be good without bad. They need each other for comparisons sake. Think about it: if things were never bad, how would we know when things are good?[22]

The point is that it is impossible to use positive thinking to completely create or manifest a "positive" reality devoid of issues or challenges. That is probably a good thing. If we are here on Earth to learn (and why are we here, if not to learn?), then the challenges are what help us to grow.

That being said, I firmly believe our desires do come true, with certain caveats, of course. Under the yogic laws of karma, it is taught that we continue to live out our desires here on earth over and over again until we realize what we are doing and transcend the karmic cy-

---

[22] I've gotten into this discussion frequently. What is the point of trying to make things better or to evolve if "bad" will always exist? I imagine that as we evolve the good/bad continuum itself might be elevated so that "bad" in an elevated realm is more like "mediocre" in our current realm. So maybe there can still be a continuum of "good" and "bad" but good is really good and bad isn't all that bad. At any rate, if all things were always the ultimate-best-good at all times, then we wouldn't know it, because we would have no frame of reference.

cle. If that is true (and many wise philosophers and saints teach that it is) our desires have to come true eventually; if not in this lifetime, then in the next. Thus ultimately, we really can have everything we desire.

So the secret of "The Secret" is this: manifesting takes patience and detachment from the ultimate form the desire will take. In my experience, our desires always come true, just not always in the timeline or form that we expect. Leaving space for possibilities is a way of remaining open to life and miraculous possibilities, while maintaining a level of detachment about the time and form our desires might take, and without resorting to blind faith or false positivity.

If we are open to the form our desires might take, we don't need to know all the steps to achieving our dreams. We only have to know the next step.

It's like the "Underpants Gnomes" episode of South Park. Have you seen that one?

Little gnomes steal one of the boy's underwear at night. When the boys catch them, the gnomes teach them about business and goal-setting. The gnomes explain that Phase 1 of their 3-step business plan is to steal underpants; and Phase 3 is profit.

Phase 2 is a blank stare. No one knows or talks about Phase 2. All the underpants gnomes know is Phase 1 and Phase 3.

Let's look at an example. Using underpants gnomes' logic, if I want to own and live at a forest retreat in the woods (and I do), that is Phase 3. I could get caught up in all the details of how I am going to make that happen, but the details are Phase 2 and Phase 2 is not really important at this moment.

Instead, I can focus on finishing the projects around my current house that need to get done before we can sell or rent it, which is something that has to happen if I am going to live in the forest. Working on the current house is Phase 1 because that has to be done regardless of how or when the forest retreat desire is going to come to fruition.

I have noticed that when I undertake Phase 1 of any desire, no matter how remote it may seem from the desire's Phase 3, doors and circumstances start to open up in my life. It's like the Universe wants to help, but its forced to wait until I take the first steps, no matter how small those steps may be.

The underpants gnomes' three-phase plan logic has been a useful tool to me on my personal spiritual quest. Leave space for the possibility that it, along with other tools you discover on your journey, will help you rediscover life's Magic, the magic we felt and believed in so freely as children.

CHAPTER 10

Magic is Magic

He is inside every being and yet He is outside too. He is far away and right here now. He moves and yet he doesn't move. It is so subtle, it is incomprehensible.

~ The Bhagavad Gita

...

[The Force is] an energy field created by all living things. It surrounds us and penetrates us; it binds the galaxy together.

~ Obi-Wan Kenobi, Star Wars

When I was a kid, I believed in magic.

I believed my stuffed animals would come to life if I wished hard enough, that my aunt and uncle's dog was my cousin, and that if you planted a pine cone and took a nap, an hour later a small pine tree will have grown in that spot, among other things.

My parents and other beloved relatives and grow-ups told me stories that encouraged and stoked my belief in magic, including the legends of Santa, the Tooth Fairy, and the Easter Bunny.

At some point, when I learned that my aunt and uncle's dog wasn't really my cousin, that my Dad planted the pine tree while a took a nap, and that Santa Claus and his gang weren't real, that all came crashing down.

I stopped believing in any magic at all, and my life was a lot more somber and pessimistic as a result.

Now I believe in a new kind of magic; the magic of synchronicities and signs and symbols and metaphors and intuition. And also sometimes just outright unexplained magic.

Like when an animal seems to communicate telepathically, or with symbols and metaphors.

It is funny, when I was a kid, I wished on every dandelion, wishbone, and eyelash that my stuffed animals would come to life and talk to me.

As I grew up, I realized that was impossible in the way that I imagined it. But it's interesting, as I've grown in my own spiritual journey, and opened myself up to the magic of possibilities and synchronicities, I have come to "talk" to animals in other ways.

So my stuffed teddy couldn't literally come to life and be my best friend. But now, I get to experience the magic of communing with animals and insects and trees, sometimes in ways where it actually seems like real freaking magic.

Like when I was introduced to cedar trees while camping in St. Augustine, Florida. We went on a nature hike and read all about the cedar trees in the area. Cedar has been used in spiritual rituals for thousands of years and cedar trees are symbolic as gateways into higher realms.

I got to meet some cedar trees while walking in a nature-induced-Zen-calm-type state of mind. I touched my hands to their bark and hugged their trunks and told them how beautiful they were.

A few days later, upon returning home, I was practicing *bhajan*[23] in my usual nature spot. After I was finished, I cut across a field that I had cut across many, many times before. This time, as I was passing a tree I

---

[23] *Bhajan* is devotional form of meditation, where one chants or sings Sanskrit yoga mantras. See the Mantra Quest in the Appendix, if you'd like to try it!

had probably passed by unnoticed hundreds of times, I felt as though someone or something grasped me.

I turned around and looked, and whether by will of wind or nature or spirit (or all three), I saw that one of the tree's branches had reached out and "grabbed" me. Gazing upward, I noticed for the first time a magnificent cedar tree. I had never noticed that cedar tree before my St. Augustine trip, even though I had passed it countless times before that day. I laughed and said hello (and gave her a big hug, of course).

I realized through my encounter with that cedar that there is an intelligence to trees that is communal: you meet and befriend one cedar, you've befriended them all. Likewise, if you have befriended one tree or plant or animal or insect of any kind, you have befriended them all, in my experience.

It is sort of like the following subtitled conversation from the movie, "Anchorman." This conversation occurred between Ron Burgundy's dog, Baxter, and a bear that was poised to attack the people that fell into its enclosure at the zoo:

> [said through a series of barks and growls between Baxter and the bear]
> Baxter: Leave these people alone. They mean you no harm.

Bear: We Bears are a proud race. They must pay for their intrusion.

Baxter: On my journey I met one of your kind. His name was Katow-jo. We became friends.

Bear: Katow-jo is my cousin. Go in peace.

Baxter: I will tell tales of your compassion.

Bear: Fare thee well, Baxter. You shall always be friend of the bears.

On second thought, maybe it's not exactly like Anchorman, but the gist is this: befriend Nature, and Nature notices.

Nature is magical, and can be a gateway into the perception of oneness; into that sense of "there is something greater than me at work that I am a part of." We often lose that sense somewhere during childhood, when we realize that some of the magic we believed in isn't actually real.

We have got to come up with a better way of making that transition from believing that our stuffed animals might come to life into the reality of adulthood, without completely crushing our openness to perceiving the magic of life.

The magic of life as an adult isn't always as overt as the magic we imagined as children. In my experience, it is subtler and quiet, often coming by way of our intuition. When we are able to tune into it, life is magical and Jedi-like.

When we learn to trust it, it is a way of triumphing over the doubting voice in our heads. For example, if brain-voice starts insisting to me that I should be doing something other than what I am doing at this moment, I tune into my heart center and ask the question: Is it ok to be doing what I am doing right now?

With practice, I have found a clear sense of "yes" or "no" and I go with it.[24] It's all I can do, right? If I am supposed to be doing something different, I must believe I would know in my heart. And if I wouldn't know, how can I be expected to do it? All I can do is live according to my level of enlightenment at this moment and continue to grow and evolve.

Everything that happens in my life is part of that journey. "Negative" circumstances aren't punishment for choosing incorrectly, but learning experiences in my personal evolutionary quest.

So how do we tune into our intuitions? There are a plenitude of practices that help us get into that space of listening and tuning into our hearts. We can choose which practices work best for us. I love my yoga mantra (or *bhajan*) practice. Also, being in nature gets me there.

---

[24] Check out the Yes/No Quest in the Appendix to try it for yourself.

And the *karmic* yoga practice of connecting with the attitude of divine service—no matter how seemingly mundane the activity. Listening and noticing is key.

There are also practices, called "*tapas*" in yoga-speak, that help to burn up impurities on an energetic level and make it easier to get into that intuitive space with less effort. These practices focus on the energy system of the body, and can seem kind of "out there" to the rational mind. I happen to be rationally-minded. I had to be rationally-minded in order to succeed as an attorney. I'm also highly intuitive and emotionally sensitive.

At times, it has felt that these two parts of me were at odds with one another, most often with my rational mind questioning my intuitive mind. But when magical, unexplainable, and unexpected things start happening over and over, eventually the rational mind has to give in. Over time, I have found, the two parts become more integrated and I have felt much more comfortable trusting my heart-yes.

One such magical-unexplainable-unexpected experience happened for me after about a month of dedicated *tapas*. I was practicing Mysore-style Ashtanga Yoga, which is a style of yoga *asana* that focuses on the subtle energy body, making it a chakra-opening-type practice. After about thirty (30) days of practicing daily, one night

I went to bed without any pomp and circumstance. Just an ordinary night.

I awoke around 3:00 AM to a distinct blue glow throughout the house. There was also the strong, clear smell of dark blue Fiddlestick markers. I think it was the smell that actually woke me up and not the glow.

Do you remember those markers? They were popular in elementary schools in the '80s. They were thin magic markers and each color had a strong, fruity smell. Orange smelled like oranges, red was cherry, and blue was, well, blue. Kind of like blue-raspberry (which, now that I think about it, is not an actual fruit).

I hadn't smelled that smell or even thought about it since I was 8 years old. And here I was, awakened in the middle night to the overwhelming smell of dark blue Fiddlestick markers, without any discernible source.

I got up out of bed and followed the blue light into the living room. On the very top shelf of the bookshelf, I noticed a wicker basket was glowing blue. I pulled it down. Inside there was a squishy ball in the shape of an eye, about the size of a baseball. I had picked it up from a vendor at a lawyer convention months prior. It was marketing schwag with the name of some company on the back of it. When you squished it, it lit up blue. I had thrown that ball up into that basket on the top shelf several months before and hadn't touched it since. Now it was illuminated in the middle of the night, without any obvious external contact: a glowing blue eyeball alerting me to its presence.

Even now, telling the story, my rational mind recognizes how silly it sounds. But the combination of waking up, seeing the glow, smelling the color blue and finding the glowing blue eye ball, along with the sensations I was feeling in my body and heart, made it extremely clear to me that something magical was happening. I smelled blue, and I saw blue. Dark blue is the color of the *ajna* chakra, the third-eye. All that *tapas* I had been doing must have been working on an energetic level in my body and I was experiencing some sort of opening.

Sometimes the magical experiences are more subtle. They come in the form of signs and coincidences, songs on the radio and gut feelings - remember the movie metaphor? But one thing is extremely clear to me: working with the subtle energy level of the body and engaging in practices designed to "burn up" impurities (*tapas*) and open up the chakras can really work. I don't believe they are necessary for spiritual development, but I do think they can sure speed up the inevitable process of evolution that all of us humans are undergoing.

And as we evolve and grow and burn up the old beliefs and judgments that cloud our perceptions, we become more open to life's magic. We can again connect with those sensations of wonder that came so easily to us as children when we believed in real magic. It is with the help of this magic and sense of wonder that we can become empowered to enter the shadow and overcome the darkness.

CHAPTER 11

Into the Shadow

Phil Connors: What would you do if you were stuck in one place and every day was exactly the same, and nothing that you did mattered?
Ralph: That about sums it up for me.

~ Groundhog Day

...

One thing remains: Vader. You must confront Vader. Then, only then, a Jedi will you be.

~ Yoda, Return of the Jedi

On the Quest, it is absolutely necessary to enter into the darkness.

We must face our fears so that we can truly open up to our most authentic selves.

That is, the hero must fight her inner tiger and find her own truth; she must face the dark side of the Force, enter the cave of evil, and recover her Light.

In real life this is an internal battle, where we face and integrate our tigers and demons so that our true Self shines through. This is a form of *svadhyaya*, the yogic concept of self-study.

In the Bhagavad Gita, this internal struggle to confront and integrate our shadow side is referred to metaphorically as the Battle of Kurukshetra. The battle metaphor is an apt one because we must be brave in the face of our fears and we must channel our inner warriors.

However, the metaphor is limited because we do not "kill" our tigers or demons, which are the parts of us we don't want to face. Instead, we acknowledge them and integrate them into ourselves so that we may become whole.

One of the eight limbs of yoga practice is *pratyahara*. *Pratyahara* is generally translated as "sense withdrawal," although in my experience of it, it is deeper than the literal withdrawing of the senses. Instead, when we practice *pratyahara*, we begin to notice in what ways our senses and feelings are drawn outward.

For example, we may notice that we are constantly getting triggered by a certain person or situation.

Whenever we think about it, we become angry and agitated. Instead of looking for a solution outward, by trying to "fix" the situation or person, we look inward to the root of the anger. We see that its root is inside, and that the person or situation almost becomes an excuse to "feel" this anger that we have been harboring inside. We practice *pratyahara* by asking ourselves in what ways we are doing the things we perceive others are doing to us. By practicing *pratyahara* in this way and reflecting on it, we are also engaging in self-study or *svadhyaya*.

We may start to notice certain Groundhog-Day-like scenarios in our lives that play out in similar fashion over and over again. We may have the same drama again and again with our spouse, our parents, our boss, or co-workers, without even realizing that the answer lies not in changing our spouse, our parents, our boss, or co-workers, but in realizing the lesson those dramas are trying to teach us about our relationship with ourselves.

In my experience, the people might even change, but the dramas stay the same. For example, I had three different jobs where I butted heads with an over-zealous office manager before realizing that I was in some ways attracting that drama so that I could learn the lessons I needed to learn from it. The players and situations changed slightly over time but the Groundhog-Day-like scenario stayed the same until *I* was ready to change.

But my biggest Groundhog Day drama involved a story that I have played out with my closest female friends a few times over my life going back to high school.

The story would go like this: I would fall in love with my best friend. I would then start to place expectations on the relationship as to how she should act, because that is how I would act, if I were her.

When she did not act the way I would act, I would tell myself that she must not love me the same way as I love her. Those thoughts would make me jealous and angry. I would get upset and withdrawn and start to act differently. The voice in my head would say, "If she doesn't feel the same way about me, why should I do all this for her?"

Then I would start to do what I blamed her for doing: I started acting in a non-loving way. I'm the one that was being an asshole, but to my brain she was the asshole for not acting the way I wanted her to act.

I finally took a closer look at it when I had an epiphany about the Groundhog-Day-esque nature of it all. By that I mean, I finally noticed that a similar drama was playing out again and again, and that realization prompted me to look deeper at it. I tried an exercise from Byron Katie's book, "I Need Your Love—Is That True?"

In it, she recommends writing a letter to the person that you are angry with. In the letter, first you apologize for three things that you did to that person, and ask if there is anything you can do to make it better. Then you thank the person for three things, tell them you love them, and close the letter.

It may seem difficult to apologize to someone you are angry at. You might have to dig deep to really find something sincere you can apologize for, especially when you probably believe that they owe you an apology. You can give them the letter or not after writing it. The big shift comes after you re-write the letter to yourself, which we will get to in a minute.

I first wrote the letter to Jessica, my current best-friend-Groundhog-Day-drama partner. It was easy to start with her, because I was still so angry with her. A voice in my head told me to write it to my mother, but I wasn't quite ready for that yet. Start with the person that's easiest, Byron Katie recommends.

I wrote a sincere apology to Jessica. I saw how our relationship failure was in part due to my personal Groundhog Day drama, and my unfulfilled expectations of how a best friend "should act." I also saw how going through the ordeal that we had gone through had taught me a lot, and had already really helped me to evolve and be a better person. I wrote:

> *Dear Jessica –*
>
> *I've realized now that I've always wanted something from you. I wanted you to be the person I wanted you to be, rather than just letting you be yourself.*
>
> *I see how I've used guilt and withdrawal of my love and energy to try to manipulate you into acting the way I wanted you to act. In so doing, I was not a good friend to you. A good friend would let you be who you are. If there is anything I can do to make it up to you, please let me know. I am deeply sorry.*
>
> *I also want to thank you for teaching me to be a better friend; for showing me what unconditional love looks like; and for being my greatest teacher over these past two-and-a-half years. Our relationship has been like a magic mirror—revealing to me hidden parts of myself— parts I didn't want to acknowledge existed—and bringing those parts into the light. I love you, Jessica, and I am eternally grateful for our time together.*
>
> *With deepest love and gratitude*
> *Kelli*

After I wrote it, it became clear that it was really about my mother. All that was wrong with my mom relationship was seeping into my other relationships—with Jessica—with everybody. I was just so annoyed to have my mother. It seemed we had so much trouble understanding each other.

I thought to myself, "Why would I have *this* mother!? She is so different than me."

The next thought came, as if from outside of myself: "Why *would* you have this mother?

Then it became clear. She is here to teach me, and I have been acting like a jerk, putting expectations on her about how a mother "should" act. And now I could finally perceive what it must have been like for her to have *me* as a daughter! We each had our own unfulfilled expectations of the relationship. I re-wrote the letter for her:

Dear Mom –

I've realized now that I've always wanted something from you. I wanted you to be the person I wanted you to be, rather than just letting you be yourself.

I see how I've used guilt and withdrawal of my love and energy to try to manipulate you into acting the way I wanted you to act. In so doing, I was not a good daughter to you. A good daughter would let you be yourself. If there is anything I can do to make it up to you, please let me know. I am deeply sorry.

I also want to thank you for teaching me to be a better person; for showing me what unconditional love looks like; and for being my greatest teacher over my life. Our relationship has been like a magic mirror—revealing to me hidden parts of myself—parts I didn't want to acknowledge existed—and bringing those parts into the light. I love you, Mom, and I am eternally grateful for our time on earth together.

With deepest love and gratitude
Kelli

And I knew I needed to give it to her; that I really owed her an apology and that she would genuinely receive it. And it was so true: she really had been my first and greatest teacher in this life. So I did. Our relationship has improved ten-fold since that day. But it really wasn't about her either...

The letter was about me.

It was me that I needed to apologize to. All the things I was doing to others—that I was blaming others for doing to me—I was also doing to myself. Byron Katie says to re-write the letter to yourself after you write it to the person you are maddest at. Basically, you just tweak it where necessary for it to make sense. This is the most important step. It is not necessary to write two letters before you re-write it for yourself, even though that is what I did. For most people, one letter to the person they are maddest at, followed by a letter to themselves will do nicely. Here is the version I re-wrote for myself:

Dear Kelli —

I've realized now that I've always wanted something from you. I wanted you to be the person I wanted you to be, rather than just letting you be yourself.

I see how I've used guilt and withdrawal of my love and energy to try to manipulate you into acting the way I wanted you to act. In so doing, I was not a good friend to you. If there is anything I can do to make it up to you, please let me know. I am deeply sorry.

I also want to thank you for teaching me to be a better human; for showing me what unconditional love looks like; and for being my greatest teacher over countless lifetimes. It's been like a magic mirror for me—revealing to me hidden parts of myself—parts I didn't want to acknowledge existed—and bringing those parts into the light. I love you, Kelli, and I am eternally grateful to you.

With deepest love and gratitude
Kelli

And the letter was so true: I wasn't letting *me* be *me*. I used guilt as a form of self-manipulation to get myself to act a certain way, the way I thought I *should* act. How is that kind to myself? And I also realized that I was really so grateful for experiencing life in this incarnation as *Kelli*. I mean, being Kelli is pretty dope, after all.

And through this incarnation, being Kelli has taught me to be a better human and to realize unconditional love. I have always been my own greatest teacher—the real me—my soul—my highest Self - the part that shows me and teaches me through my projections onto others and through my life situations and karma. Wow. It was really cathartic.

I felt a huge shift in my life after I wrote those three letters.

In a lot of ways, that was my cave of darkness. I had to confront my shadow side and see that the anger I was projecting onto others (again and again like a Groundhog Day) wasn't really about them at all.

We tend to play out our Groundhog Day stories time and again until we wake up to the lessons they contain. Our family members and those closest to us are often the source of our misplaced emotions until we look deeper.

And what a gift they give us; those people close to us that drive us nuts and push our buttons. They help us to see and realize our true Selves. They are our true guides and teachers on our quests, even if they are not consciously aware of it.

CHAPTER 12

We are Family

If you think you're enlightened, go spend a week with your family.

~ Ram Dass

...

No, I am your father.

~ Darth Vader, <u>Empire Strikes Back</u>

Family relationships are invaluable tools for learning on the quest and are ripe for self-study and *pratyahara* practice.

That is both because our relationships with our family and partners can be our biggest triggers and greatest teachers, and because of the deep soul connections I believe we share. Family members have a way of getting under our skin like no one else; but those relationships are also the deepest and most rewarding. Family includes our blood family and also our partners and close friends that become like family.

I've heard it said that when one reaches enlightenment, seven generations of one's family—both forward and backward—also attain enlightenment. I could see how that is true—in my experience our karma is deeply linked with that of our family. We seem to inherit versions of our parent's karmic issues. Our personal "Groundhog Day" dramas might be deeply tied to our issues with our parents, which are typically similar to issues our parents had with their parents. We seem to pass on these karmas from generation to generation and when we are able to break free of our own personal Groundhog Day, perhaps we stop passing it on to our children.

It is probably for that very reason that our parents (in particular) and other family members can be our biggest emotional triggers.

If you feel particularly triggered by certain family members, in addition to exploring *pratyahara*-type practices like Byron Katie's Apology Letter exercise described in the last chapter, my recommendation is to channel your inner sociologist or anthropologist. Treat family gatherings like Jane Goodall would study chimpanzees: with curiosity and wonder.

Watch the interactions while staying slightly removed from the action. Imagine you are taking notes and commenting, as if narrating a nature documentary. You wouldn't try to change or interfere with the chimpanzees in their native habitat would you? But learning about their tendencies and motivations would be truly fascinating.

Remember that curiosity defeats judgment. By that I mean, rather than reacting to judgment with judgment, ask questions and practice active listening. Try to understand the life experiences and personal tendencies that have made our family members into who they are with their own individual beliefs and patterns.

Ram Dass, the great spiritual teacher, said to see people as trees; each unique and beautiful in their own way and with no need for us to place our judgments and expectations upon them. He said:

> That when you go out into the woods and you look at trees, you see all these different trees. And some of them are bent, and some of them are straight, and some of them are evergreens, and some of them are whatever. And you look at the tree and you allow it. You appreciate it. You see why it is the way it is. You sort of understand

that it didn't get enough light, and so it turned that way. And you don't get all emotional about it. You just allow it. You appreciate the tree.

The minute you get near humans, you lose all that. And you are constantly saying "You're too this, or I'm too this." That judging mind comes in. And so I practice turning people into trees. Which means appreciating them just the way they are.

I would not want to make an apple tree into an oak; instead, I can enjoy the apple tree for what it is. The same with family. I can enjoy Uncle John for who he is and understand that his opinions and beliefs are a result of his unique make-up and life experiences and have nothing to do with his spiritual Essence, which is as beautiful as a majestic oak.

I like to think we make soul-pacts with our family members before we come to Earth. We agree that we are here for each other's highest learning, no matter what the cost. If we treat our closest relationships as learning tools, then we will progress quickly on our quests.

Because of my personal experience of these strong soul connections and pacts we share with those closest to us, I firmly believe that loved ones that have left this Earth still very often offer guidance and assistance in the forms of signs, coincidences, and dreams. And the more we are open to listening to their guidance, the more often it is available to us. This is another invaluable tool on our personal quests.

I had a dream about my Dad after he passed. We were swimming together in strong white water rapids and coming up on a huge, spine-chilling wall of water. We kept getting closer and closer to the wall and we looked at each other with enthusiastic determination and said, "let's do this!"

We dove right in and swam with all our might and we made it across the frightening, waterfall-like rapids. We turned around and looked back at the wall as the rapids carried us more slowly down stream. We saw that there was actually a much easier way to traverse the water-wall: You could simply go under it to the calm water and not get as battered and bruised. We had done it the hard way, but now we could see there was an easier way to tell others behind us about.

My Dad was teaching me, through this dream, that my experiences might be a little rough, but part of the reason for that is so that I can make it easier for the others that follow me. We used to joke when he was alive that his motto was "why do when you can overdo?" Whatever he did, he went for it with passion, and I take after him in that regard.

Another time, more recently he clearly assisted me in my waking life. I walked by the bookshelf in my house containing the large volume of books he had left me when he died.

A book about St. Teresa caught my eye. I picked it up and started reading it. It was a biography about her. It was interesting, but I couldn't get into it. I had the thought that I'd really like to read something *she* wrote about her own spiritual journey; rather than this dry-ish, scholarly work, written by someone about her. I put the book away.

About a week later at my mom's house, my mom directed me to a box of books from my Dad. It was one that she had overlooked five years earlier, when she had given me all the books he had left me. I took the box home, opened it up, and guess what was right on top? St. Teresa's "Interior Castle," her seminal work about her personal experiences of the divine.

Inside was a bookmark from an ashram I had visited with my Dad right before he died. I instantly knew that he had been reading this very book when he died! It even had some of his handwritten notes in the margins.

That book was exactly what I needed on my path at that moment, and receiving it felt like a direct response from my dad to my unspoken desire to learn more about St. Teresa. Hearing St. Teresa describe her own ups and downs in her quest validated my own experiences. I gained insight into mystical spiritual experiences from someone who shared my religious upbringing: Catholicism.

A few weeks later my mom saw me carrying the book around and recognized it. She pointed to it and said, "wasn't that the book your dad reading when he died?" More validation.

These signs and coincidences from loved ones can happen even more subtly and simply. Often times I'll hear a song that reminds me of Dad or Daniel or Grandma Teddy at exactly the right moment. Survivor's "Eye of the Tiger" always makes me thing of Daniel. Or I'll see a firefighter sticker on the back of a car, or Miami Hurricanes logo and know that Dad (a career firefighter) and Daniel (a lifelong 'Canes fan) are with me.

All of these experiences have led me to perceive that it is only a person's physical body that leaves the Earth when we die. There is a subtle spirit that remains. In a lot of ways, this spirit is even better: it can be accessed by anyone, from anywhere at any time, even by multiple different people in different locations at the same moment; it is the flawless, highest, most perfect version of the person; none of the earthly flaws our loved ones had remain—just their spiritual essence; their own personal brand of the Divine. They become like their own arche-types and they are omnipresent.

This is probably why ancient humans worshipped their ancestors. They could perceive that the spiritual essence of their mothers and fathers remained after their bodies has died. I believe this is why one of the ten commandments is to "honor thy father and mother."[25]

There is a reason we are born into the families we are born into. We are karmically connected to each other and bound to help one another on our evolutionary quests. One invaluable tool on our quests is to tap into this ancestor wisdom; it will help lead us to freedom.

---

[25] Exodus 20:12

IV. Freedom

Karma asukla akrsnam yoginah trividham itaresam

"the actions of a true yogi are neither white nor black; for others, their actions are either white or black or mixed."

~ Sutra IV, 7, <u>The Yoga Sutras of Patanjali</u>

CHAPTER 13

Freedom

Power said to the world, "You are mine."
The world kept it prisoner on her throne.
Love said to the world, "I am thine."
The world gave it the freedom of her house."

~ Rabindranath Tagore

...

"One fighter with a sharp stick, with nothing left to lose, can win the day."

~ Jyn Erso, <u>Rogue One</u>

Freedom doesn't come from outside; nor is it dependent on people or circumstances.

Freedom flows naturally when the desire to live openly and authentically overcomes any fears of loss.

Freedom comes from inside. No one can control our freedom; it is up to us. We often place blame on people or circumstances in our outside world when we feel caged—when we feel a lack of freedom.

But the real freedom comes by allowing yourself to be you. It's a letting go of self-judgment. It's a letting go of the mental judgments and attitudes holding us back from becoming what we are.

Self-freedom is not so much a freedom to do whatever we want. It is not to be confused with callousness; it's not an attitude of "I do what I want" without any thought of the repercussions.

Instead, it's a freedom to think and feel and *be* without the self-judgment. It is an allowing of ourselves to be who we are, even when society, family, or other perceived outside pressures might want us to be something else. We cannot control outside judgment, but we can control our own inner judgment. The truth is that outside judgments only hurt when there is an inner judgment to go along with it. Without a corresponding inner judgment, I've noticed that outside judgments roll right off my back and are often even humorous.

When we allow ourselves to be who we are without self-judgment, then we are really free. We are free to be our authentic selves. When we embody our most authentic selves, we often find that the perceived outside forces that we believed were limiting our freedom fall away naturally without force or coercion.

Being honest with yourself about who you are enables you to live your truth, to live authentically, even when you think that doing so might result in loss. It's living your *dharma*, your soul purpose, without fear.

Janis Joplin sang that "freedom is just another word for nothing left to lose." And what do we really ever have to lose that is rightfully ours to begin with? If the only way to keep what we fear to lose is by living a lie—or even a half-truth—then we are doomed to live a very unfulfilling, stressful existence. We live a lie when we are dishonest with ourselves and others about who we really are; when we refuse to acknowledge our stories.

Scholar Brene Brown says, "When we deny our stories, they define us. When we own our stories, we get to write a brave new ending."

In other words, in owning our truth and choosing to live authentically, even if that truth may be different from what friends and family expect of us, we get to be involved in co-creating the ending to our story.

That is what happened to me with the Jessica Groundhog Day drama. I had to realize my story; I had to realize what I was doing and own it before I got to write a brave new ending. And it was scary to do that. It was scary to be honest about who I truly was. Part of that for me involved owning an aspect of my sexuality I had never brought into the light before: I was capable of falling into romantic love not just with men but also with women. I had pushed that part of myself deep down and that was part of the reason I was repeating similar dramas again and again.

I had to own up to my story to my partner, my husband, and risk that he might not appreciate that revelation. I am grateful that he is extraordinary and accepts me for me, even though I am not exactly who either of us thought I was when we got married. The truth is that we all change over time, in varying degrees. It is important to own it, rather than trying to continue to be an old version of ourselves when that path no longer serves us.

The alternative is far worse: in my life, living a half-truth was creating emotional turmoil that was wreaking havoc in many other ways. I had to own who I was and face the consequences; I had to risk loss in order to live with freedom and authenticity.

If I hadn't, I would have continued to attract circumstances and dramas that caused me suffering. That is how life works, in my experience. Suffering is definitely a path to enlightenment, though I think there is an easier way.

It's like the dream I had with my Dad where we realized there was an easier way to cross the tumultuous waterfall-like rapids: there is an easier way than the path of suffering, although suffering will get you there. I think the key is having the intention and desire to grow and evolve. We really have to desire awakening and put some passion into it. We have to heed the call of our heart and intuition and take action when necessary. Complacency won't do.

That is why suffering has been the path of choice for humans for a while: it is easy to be complacent when life is status quo and things are ok, but not great. It is harder to be complacent when we are suffering and our lives our falling apart. So if our souls are on the fast-track toward awakening, we may notice that we continue to suffer until we consciously undertake a journey to change.

But we can make a decision today to set forth on our own personal quest for freedom and authenticity, and not wait for crappy circumstances to force us into a state of seeking answers the hard way. Instead, we can practice techniques and mini-quests like those discussed in this book, and start out on our own personal journeys right now.

The good news is; we don't have to change everyone. There'll be people on Earth that are not ready to live fearlessly and with freedom, authenticity, and open hearts. We can nonetheless help them as we work on ourselves: by being living examples, and by exuding that state of connectedness and open-heartedness with such magnitude, it's impossible for those around us not to feel it and react positively to it.

Ancient civilizations were able to recognize that feeling that comes when we are acting in alignment with our highest Selves. I believe that is how great structures like Stonehenge, the pyramids, and the Mayan ruins were probably built.

We've lost sight of that, and we tend to rely on the most external level of reality that's associated with the physical senses rather than relying on a deeper more internal sense of reality.

But we can reconnect with that innermost sense, our instinct. And it feels amazing to connect with that sensation.

We teach our kids to push that down. We teach them to be responsible, to obey, to get a good job, and to pay the bills and be stressed out. If instead we were to teach them to connect with their own inner wisdom and to feel compassion and love for everyone and everything, we would have a whole new race of humans—ones that probably wouldn't need to rely on jobs at all.

There is a theory that we will soon to reach singularity, where humans and computers are indistinguishable, like the Elon Musk computer simulation idea we discussed earlier. What that could mean is that we will eventually get to a point where technology is so advanced that we can instantly solve the world's problems, like pollution and hunger. We can envision a future where traditional jobs are completely unnecessary. People will be more free to invest time in higher pursuits that speak to their souls.

Or maybe it means the robot aliens will take over and we will become their slaves as they strip our planet of its resources to serve their own egomaniacal extraterrestrial motives.

I'm not totally clear. I'm a lawyer, not a scientist.

But the point is that we suffer here on Earth mostly at the hands of our own limiting beliefs, and we pass those beliefs on to our children. What if we were evolve to a point where we no longer held onto limiting thoughts and we were able to connect with and work for the greater good of the whole of humanity?

I sometimes wonder why our souls chose to live in this realm. It's a realm of suffering. The Bhagavad Gita refers to it as "a world of misery and transitory existence."[26] I suppose that it might be one of the lower realms, and I imagine that there are realms where manifested beings realize their true nature faster and suffer less at the hands of their own limiting beliefs.

I think the flipside of the suffering and the real attraction of this realm is the humor and grit that comes along with the unique perspective that living on Earth as a human beings. I'm not sure the higher realms are quite as funny or endearing. (Or have sushi or Sauternes or poker.)

At the end (or was it?) of my story I realized that I had pretty much bottomed out. Things had gotten worse than I could've imagined. I experienced tragedy in the forms of the deaths of my Dad and Daniel. Then I experienced deep heartbreak at the hands of my Jessica story almost immediately thereafter. That trajectory of my life path really helped me to understand better the true nature of devotion and oneness.

When you get to a point where things are about as bad or worse than you could've ever imagined, and you survive and you are okay, you realize that you will be okay no matter what happens.

There's a fearlessness and freedom that comes with that realization.

---

[26] Chapter 8:15

Nonetheless, we do not have to wait for deep suffering in order to live with authenticity and freedom.

And if we don't want to suffer, then the sooner we can start to live our truth now, the better.

CHAPTER 14

Red Light Camera Story

Be so good they can't ignore you.

~ Steve Martin

...

Many of the beliefs you cling to depend greatly on your point of view.

~ Obi Wan Kenobi

When we live our truth we become a living example, exuding an energy of interconnectedness and open-heartedness with such magnitude that it's impossible to ignore.

We start to attract circumstances and people that are in alignment with our goals and our ability to effect change becomes even greater.

Sometimes living our truth is as simple as heeding that little feeling that is telling us to take action even when the judging-brain-voice kicks in with negative feedback to the contrary.

That is what happened to me when I decided to fight my red light camera (RLC) ticket.

Have you heard about those? It is a ticket, sent to you in the mail, after an out-of-state, private vendor takes a picture of your car "running" a red light. One big problem is that the system isn't set up to make people safer, it is set up to make money. In fact, in Florida, rear-end collisions and accidents with incapacitating injuries have increased significantly since RLCs were allowed in the state.[27]

Yellow light times are set purposely low in order to create a situation where drivers end up running red lights by fractions of a second. My ticket was for running a red light by .2 seconds. But the biggest problem with RLCs is that it is against the edicts of our federal

---

[27] See the "Florida Department of Highway Safety, Red Light Camera Summary Reports, Fiscal Years 2014-15 and 2015-16."

and state constitutions to allow a private company to essential step into the shoes of the local police force.

There are other problems with the red light camera system too, but I don't want to get myself too fired up about it here. The point is I decided to fight my ticket. There is an old adage, "the lawyer that represents herself has a fool for a client." I had my doubts about using my precious time to fight the system, but in the end my instinct prevailed.

That decision to fight my RLC ticket sent my life on an interesting trajectory. I really expected to lose my case but I ended up winning and becoming kinda-sorta-locally-niche famous. I gave at least a dozen television interviews to local and non-local news, and I even did a radio spot.

I got to see a bit of the ugly side of fame—the trolls and the lack of privacy.

It was mostly positive feedback and congratulations after my win, which felt awesome. My case set an important precedent and helped many others with their own RLC challenges. It turns out red light cameras are an issue that is non-partisan, and most people I've encountered—whether generally conservative or liberal—come together in their disdain for RLCs. It is like we inherently sense that it is unfair to get a ticket from a camera rather than a real live police officer.

But I wasn't expecting that I would encounter people who vehemently disagreed with me and who had no problem screaming at me that I was wrong, or making negative comments about my looks, or telling me that I should "burn in a lake of fire because I must be queer."

I had to resist the temptation to devolve into engaging the naysayers at their level. It would be counterproductive to try to argue with someone who is saying mean things by saying mean things back. It certainly won't do anything to change that person's mind or the minds of anyone else who might be reading their comments.

That is where my lawyerly wisdom kicked in. To be effective, lawyers must know how to maintain courtesy and professionalism while engaging in passionate discourse. Being a lawyer taught me how to separate people from their arguments. And being a yogi helped me to stay calm and not let my anger get the best of me.

As we discussed in Chapter 4, we can admonish a person's actions or beliefs without attacking the person themselves. We can separate people from their arguments in our mind, so that any frustration we feel is directed not at the person but at the argument.

We, as humans, have to learn to rise up and engage in discourse without devolving into personal attacks, even when we are personally under attack. We do this by realizing the person we are arguing with is our brother or sister on Earth, who shares the same divine essence as us, and who has become who they are due to their unique life circumstances, choices, and moral commitments.

There is a lot of unrest in America right now between the different political extremes. But the real difference between "conservatives" and "liberals" comes down to differing moral commitments. It comes down to different ways of seeing the world that need not be at odds with each other.

In fact, conservatives and liberals need each other in order to exist. It comes back to the nature of duality we discussed in the Judgment chapter—dark cannot exist without light, nor up without down, nor conservatives without liberals—because they need each other for comparison's sake. If there were no liberals, there would be no conservatives and vice versa.

And the real difference between so-called conservatives and so-called liberals is really their driving passions and framework for morality.

The moral commitments of liberals and conservatives are divergent—typically liberals frame their moral arguments in terms of reciprocity and caring while conservatives frame their moral arguments in terms of patriotism and loyalty.[28] We tend to make arguments that are founded in terms of our own moral values, rather than the values of the person we are engaging with. But if we consciously reframe our arguments in order to appeal to the moral values of the person we are engaging, we will have a more effective discussion.

Often we are arguing apples and oranges. Reframing our arguments can help make them more effective, and can help us to better see points of view that are different from our own. But more importantly, we have to learn to see people as distinct from their beliefs and arguments. We can love and appreciate the person—or at least offer them courtesy and respect—while passionately disagreeing with the person's position. And we must strive to do this even when the person with whom we are disagreeing with is being hateful.

This becomes easier as we live our truth and heed our inner wisdom. Being committed to the quest does not mean refusing to go to battle. When it is time to take up a cause and fight, then we must do our *dharma* and fight. Like Krishna said to Arjuna, "from the perspective of dharma, you should not hesitate, since for a warrior

---

28 Feinberg, M; Willer, R., "From Gulf to Bridge: When Do Moral Arguments Facilitate Political Influence?" Personality and Social Psychology Bulletin, 41:12, 1665-1681 (October 2015).

like you there is no greater cause than to fight for dharma."[29] However, realize what it is that we are actually fighting: it is an issue or an idea—it isn't another person.

Start locally. Start by making positive changes in your own neighborhood and town. Heck start with your own body. Like Rumi said, "yesterday I was clever, so I wanted to change the world. Today I am wise, so I am changing myself."

If we can affect change at the microcosm level in our own bodies, we can affect change at the level of the macrocosm, because we are a part of a greater whole. And when we do that, by living our truths, it is a lot more difficult for the haters to hate. And in the very least, any attacks are a lot less hurt-ty when we are living with authenticity.

That we are part of a greater whole, completely inseparable from the Universe is exemplified when one looks at fractal geometry and its occurrence in nature.

Fractals are irregular patterns that repeat over and over at both the macrocosm and microcosm levels. Common examples of fractals are seashells and snow flakes and broccoli.

---

[29] Chapter 2:31

Whether you look at one under a microscope or with the naked eye, the same patterns appear. That is, whether you zoom in really close, or zoom out really far, you are looking at the same thing. The whole of a fractal looks the same as a smaller part, which is the same as an even smaller part. This is called "self-similarity" and it can be found all over nature, including on the surface of the moon and in the arteries of our hearts.

And fractals in nature can get even more astonishing. For example, it turns out that the tree density and placement in a forest is the same as the density and placement of branches on any individual tree in that forest.[30] Meaning that the spacing, placement, and thickness of branches on an individual tree is remarkably similar to the spacing, placement, and thickness of tree trunks in the whole forest; and that the relative number of big and small trees in the forest closely matches the relative number of big and small branches on an individual tree.

Fractals exist everywhere, including in our own bodies. Maybe this is why it is said that God created mankind in God's own image.[31] The Universe we can see outside of ourselves when we gaze up into the cosmos

---

[30] See, "Hunting the Hidden Dimension," PBS documentary, 2008.

[31] Genesis 1:27

looks remarkably similar to the cosmos we see at the quantum level in our bodies, like we discussed in Chapter 2. Yogis often use the metaphor that we are like the individual rays of the sun or waves on the ocean, inseparable from and yet a perfect reflection of the Whole.

In addition, we have at least as many or more bacteria and organisms living in our bodies as we have cells—this means there are more things that are "other" than us than things that are "us" in our own bodies.[32]

Therefore, it is fruitless to label things or people as "other" than us or even as "bad" or "good" when we are all part of the same Universe, and we are all reflections of the One.

I find we have a tendency to want to see things as either black or white. It's hard to exist in shades of gray. We want to know that coffee or sugar is either good for us or bad for us and not somewhere in between.

By the same token, we tend to either exaggerate the positive or overemphasize the negative—rather than just seeing reality exactly as it is. I find this tendency was at the heart of my Jessica drama.

---

[32] Sender, R; Fuchs, S; Milo, R., "Revised Estimates for the Number of Human and Bacteria Cells in the Body," PLOS Biology Journal (August 19, 2016).

We want to see people as either with us or against us; good or bad. The reality is we are all of those things and more. We are good and bad, righteous and unrighteous, divine and diabolical—all at the same the time—depending upon the vantage point. No one exists in black and white. We have to learn to live with that discomfort of not having a clear line.

We have to interact with people that we may dislike and continue to wage our battles with professional courtesy and compassion. We can be so good that we cannot be ignored, while at the same time maintaining the high road and refusing to engage haters at the level of hate.

And we can have some fun with it. I love troll-engaging. I love keeping the high road while someone else tries to pull me down with insults. I get a bizarre satisfaction from refusing to engage at that level. I find humor in trying to find some sort of colorable truth or lesson in what the negator is saying, and giving them credit when credit is due. And I have actually learned a thing or two about myself—and even about red light cameras—from those types of interactions.

It is a way to have fun with and enjoy the gritty-not-so-pretty parts of life.

Because in real life we want things to be black or white or right or wrong. We want there to be clear winners and losers. We want to see things as either working out or falling apart. But life doesn't generally happen that way.

Pema Chodron, beloved Buddhist teacher, says:

> We think that the point is to pass the test or overcome the problem, but the truth is that things don't really get solved. They come together and they fall apart. Then they come together again and fall apart again. It's just like that. The healing comes from letting there be room for all of this to happen: room for grief, for relief, for misery, for joy.

And maybe, that is the whole point of living life: to have the full range of human experience—the grief, the joy, the misery, the humor—all of it.

CHAPTER 15

Mermaid

You are the one
that longs to run
and revel in this foolish game.
No need to go
You are the flow
You leave it all to live on the land...
and Dance
with storms...
To feel...
The grit,
the glory
of sand.
~ Rotten Minerva[33]

---

[33] Inspired by Maurice Sendak's <u>Animal Family</u> and Lionel Ritchie's, "You Are."

...

Fear is the path to the dark side. Fear leads to anger. Anger leads to hate. Hate leads to suffering.

~ Yoda, The Phantom Menace

Maybe we are here, in part, to play; to enjoy the glory of being alive.

With all of its shitty awesomeness and awesome shittiness.

This is *Lila*, God's play. And to some extent, we are here to play our roles and enjoy the game.

It's like the Bill Murray flick, "The Man Who Knew too Little." His character, Wallace Ritchie, believes he is taking part in the "Theatre of Life," which is an elaborate role-playing theater experience. But he ends up in a real-life crime drama, while thinking the whole time he is simply an actor in a role. The level of detachment that comes from thinking the drama isn't real, turns Wallace into a superhero. He is able to defeat all the bad guys and save the day with hilarious ease, all because he fully commits to his role with humor, enjoyment and detachment.

There is a certain dark humor to this reality, isn't there? And there is a certain beauty in the melancholy that comes from the constant change and death we experience here. There is beauty in engaging in the full range of human experience—from the blissful to the painful.

We aren't here to deny our humanity or avoid any part of the full human experience. Even with all my talk about our inner divinity, I can't and wouldn't want to deny that we are human.

That is why the mermaid leaves the sea to live on the land—for the sheer joy of the human experience. For both the ups and downs, the pain and joy. In the wonderful children's fable, "The Animal Family," the mermaid explains life in the sea versus life on land to the hunter, her human partner:

> [The sea people] don't know how to be bored or miserable. One day is one wave, and the next day the next, for the sea people—and whether they're glad or whether they're sorry, the sea washes it away. When my sister died, the next day I'd forgotten and was happy. But if you died [the hunter], if he died [their son], my heart would break.
>
> When it storms for the [sea] people, no matter how terribly it storms, the storm isn't real—swim down a few strokes and its calm there, down there it's always calm.

And death is no different, if its someone else who dies. We say, "swim away from it"; we swim away from everything.

But on land it's different. The storm's real, here, and the red leaves and the branches when they're bare all winter. It all changes and never stops changing, and I'm here with nowhere to swim to, no way ever to leave it or forget it. No, the land's better! The land's better!

Maybe we are here to live life for the glory of life. We are here for the grit. We are here to be part of the divine play and to experience all that this world has to offer—we aren't here to avoid any part of that experience.

Maybe the real heaven is to walk on Earth, like the great Buddhist teacher Thich Nhat Hanh said in "The Miracle of Mindfulness":

People usually consider walking on water or in thin air a miracle. But I think the real miracle is not to walk either on water or in thin air, but to walk on earth. Every day we are engaged in a miracle which we don't even recognize: a blue sky, white clouds, green leaves, the black, curious eyes of a child—our own two eyes. All is a miracle.

Nature has a way of revealing this miracle to us and showing us the beauty in the full experience of this reality. Hubert Reeves said, "Man is the most insane species. He worships an invisible God and destroys a visible Nature. Unaware that this Nature he's destroying is this God he's worshiping."

I've always found solace in Nature and it has helped me to come to understand the full range of the human experience. Nature was a particularly great teacher for me during one of my adventures on my personal journey.

During the time period of my decent into my cave of darkness on my personal quest, I decided I wanted to go camping alone in the woods for at least one night. I imagined that my campsite would be secluded and surrounded by forest, with no other campers within eye or earshot, giving me a real chance to deal with whatever shadows arose within me during my time alone. I figured I would have to confront some deep-seated fears that would only dare peak out during my time of seclusion.

I was already flustered by the time I arrived at the campsite after a two-hour drive, leaving me about thirty minutes until sunset to get my tent pitched. I was immediately put on edge by the fact that the campground was not what I expected. My tent would not be secluded in the middle of the woods, but would instead be surrounded by other families of campers just a few yards away. They were all sitting around with their already-pitched tents and cozy campfires and I felt like I was in a fishbowl: it seemed like all of their eyes were on me, judging me and my tent-pitching capabilities as I tried to set up my site before sunset.

I envisioned that they were probably laughing and commenting to each other about whether or not I knew what the hell I was doing. My judging mind was already laughing and commenting to me in my own head.

I looked at the instructions to my tent (which I had set up in my backyard to practice all by myself without issue a month before). The instructions mocked me, suggesting two adults were necessary to get the main tent pole up. All I could think was, "I don't want any help! I just want to set this up and vibe out with myself and my alone time. I hope no one tries to offer me any help."

As I tried to raise up the two main tent poles crisscrossed from each other, dirt got into the bottom of the poles, preventing me from inserting the pin into the bottom of each pole. I laid down the tent and attempted to pry the dirt out with a pen. Nope. A knife? Fail.

The voices in my head were relentless. I kept imagining what the other campers were thinking about me and

I berated myself for my choice of campground, my decision to camp in the first place, for leaving late and losing daylight; for everything. I decided the only way to get the dirt out of the bottom of the poles would be to bang it out on the pavement.

I drove up to the paved parking lot at the campground entrance, the nearest pavement around. When I got to the parking lot and banged the first pole on the pavement, the elastic holding the pole together snapped, leaving my tent pole in about eight pieces.

Again with the voices and judgment. There was no readily-available way to fix it. Should I drive back home at this point? Try to find another tent? How do I always end up in these situations? I'm such an asshole.

I decided to drive into "town" to see if I could buy another tent. The grocery-like store looked promising — it might have camping equipment. Indeed, it did, but no tents. I was really anxious and tense as I walked up and down the aisles of the store. The women working there kind of looked at me funny. I had the thought that I should ask for help, but again brain voice shot me down: "I don't need any help! I don't want to ask for any help!!"

As I walked out the store, a bright-gypsy-eyed, long-haired, older woman looked up at me. I noticed the thought, "I wonder if she is a teacher? Her eyes are so knowing." Then the thought, "Nope, still not going to ask for help." I observed as I walked out the store that I was tensely clutching my huge purse with my hands in front of me, rather than over my shoulder like normal.

When I got out to my car, which was packed to the brim with food and other camping supplies, I realized my hands were shaking with hunger because I had forgotten to eat dinner. I went into the back of my car and grabbed something to eat. As I was getting the food, I put my purse in the back and all my stuff accidentally dumped out of it. I scrambled to get everything back in and get settled back into the front seat of my car to figure out what the hell I was going to do. Find a hotel? Try to buy a tent somewhere else? Drive home? While I was thinking and stuffing my grill, I saw the outline of the long-haired-teacher in my peripheral vision.

Then I realized she was reading my license tag and was writing something down. She started to head back inside. Was she writing down my license plate number? I yelled after her,

"Excuse me, ma'am, is there something I can help you with?"

"We know you were stealin'. I'm calling the police."

Oh shit. Time to fess up my need for help. I suppose I did look pretty shifty walking around, carrying my purse weird and not buying anything. "Ma'am, I wasn't stealing. I need help."

"You had something in your purse. We saw you empty it out into the back of your car."

"No, I wasn't stealing. I was getting this food out of the back of my car. I need help. I was trying to set up my tent and my tent pole broke." I showed her the broken pieces.

"Yeah that is a broken tent pole alright."

"I'll show you the back of my car." I start fumbling for my keys to open the hatch and I couldn't find them anywhere. It was like they fucking disappeared. While I looked for the keys I continued, "I was just nervous because my tent broke and I'm from out of town and I'm not sure what I am going to do tonight. You were probably picking up on my nervous energy."

She was still a little agitated. "Yeah all four of us in the store picked up on something."

I finally found my keys and opened the back for her to look around. I also opened my purse and let her look in there.

She softened. "There is nowhere to buy a tent around here. But you may be able to stay at Elite Campground up the road. They have cabins you can rent. The owners are up at Salty's tavern by this time of night, so just go into the bar there and ask around and you will find them. Are you going to be here a few days?"

"Thank you very much. Yes, I'll be here two days."

"If you come back to the store, leave your purse in the car."

Ok, sounds fair.

I left after getting directions. Perhaps not surprisingly, I completely misunderstood how to get to Salty's and ended up driving around whispering to myself about how suspicious everyone in this small town must be and again fell into a steady stream of self-deprecating thoughts related to the predicament I found myself in.

"Crucify" by Tori Amos came on the radio. I noticed it was about the fourth time in two days that I had heard that song:

Why do we
Crucify ourselves
Every day
I crucify myself
Nothing I do is good enough for you
Crucify myself
Every day
And my heart is sick of being in chains
I gotta have my suffering
So that I can have my cross
I know a cat named Easter
He says will you ever learn
You're just an empty cage girl

If you kill the bird.

I finally found Salty's by accidently driving right into the Elite campground and right up to the gatekeeper. I was very nervous when she directed me to roll down my window.

"I'm trying to find Salty's..." I started. I could hear Karaoke coming from a bar in a strip mall a hundred yards behind the gate.

"Salty's is right there," she said pointing in the direction of the Karaoke.

"Actually, I need a place to stay. I broke my tent pole, so I couldn't put my tent together, so I tried to find another tent, and the lady at the grocery store said maybe you had a cabin available here I could rent?" I was nervous and the words were rapidly spilling out of my mouth; still not sure if she was friend or foe.

"I used to have a car like this," she said, gazing at my Mini Cooper. "it was a red convertible. I drove it many years ago when I was young." Her nostalgia revealed her kindness and I instantly felt relieved.

She said, "You don't want to stay here. It's too expensive. You have to put a deposit of $100 per night down and pay $100 for the cabin per night. Why don't you just go up to the store right there and buy some duct tape and fix your tent pole?" She pointed to the Dollar General on the other side of the strip mall.

Brilliant! Duct tape! "Yes, that's great. Thank you so much!"

"And come back later for some Karaoke at Salty's once you get your tent all set up!"

So long story short, I got my tent set up in the dark by myself using the miracle of duct tape. And I am shortening the story, because by the time the ordeal was over, I was way too tired for Karaoke, despite my deep love and appreciation for the art form.

As I laid down to go to sleep that night, I could hear the other campers all around me. I laughed at how not-like-I-imagined camping was turning out to be. I wasn't alone at all. I was practically in wide-open public. Maybe that was the point—to be myself in the open. And maybe if I had asked for help from the start I wouldn't have gone through the whole predicament. But what is the fun in that?

Obviously I needed to learn something. Maybe the grocery-story-lady was a teacher after all. And what is with the constant judgment of myself? Even Tory Amos was trying to tell me something. I let my emotions rise up within me and pass.

The next day I went to make a fire before the sun came up. I couldn't see what I was doing and all of a sudden my feet were burning all over. Ants! Nuts there must have been a 100 bites.

I actually got myself still for a minute, sat in a meditative posture, and tried to connect with the ants that had just bitten me: What was the great ant spirit trying to teach me? Then I looked down and saw that I had dropped my fire wood right on top of their giant ant mound.

The great ant spirit wants your shit out of its house! Ahem, yes, maybe moving the firewood will help.

The ant bites seemed to fuel my anger. I felt like I was barfing up old anger vibes for the next several days after coming home from camping. (I had also literally barfed several times after having champagne and s'mores for dinner one camping night). But the anger vibes came in nauseating waves. I had really stirred up some fire over some old situations in my life. I realized I still had a lot of buried anger that needed out. Kind of like a demon or tiger, lurking in the deep recesses of my heart.

In my experience, my demons of un-dealt with emotions can't be pushed down or forced out. It's more like I have to sit down with them, invite them to talk to me, and listen to what they are there to teach me.

Gandhi said, "the only devils in this world are those running around in our own hearts, and that is where all our battles should be fought."

And Thick Nhat Hanh explained anger this way:

Anger is like a howling baby, suffering and crying. The baby needs his mother to embrace him. You are the mother for your baby, your anger. The moment you begin to practice breathing mindfully in and out, you have the energy of a mother, to cradle and embrace the baby. Just embracing your anger, just breathing in and breathing out, that is good enough. The baby will feel relief right away.

When an unwanted emotion arises, rather than suppress it, I invite it in, I feel it, intensify it even, and then direct it toward the Divine. This is the *bhakti* practice of devotion described in Chapter 7.

After my camping trip, my anger tigers were triggered. They didn't want to be suppressed anymore. I struggled with the urge to project the anger outward, toward friends and loved ones who had "wronged" me in some way. I also struggled with the urge to "crucify myself" and project the anger inward at all my self-perceived flaws and incapacities. I resisted, and instead, I got really mad at the Divine Mother.

Why do you insist on putting me in these situations with these assholes that make me angry? Why do you have to make me so scatter-brained and crazy? Why do I seem to live the same damn stories over and over again, no matter how I struggle to try to change them? Why I am surrounded by assholes? Why am I such an asshole? The anger inside me welled up and was released in a several fits of tears and rage over several days.

With that release came more joy and a sense of lightness and humor when viewing my stories in the light of day. Mother Nature sure has some darkly humorous ways of teaching me. I am not sure I would want it any other way. I love the dirt and grit and pain and beauty of the full range of human experience.

There is a reason the mermaid wanted to come here, even though she could have stayed safely home in the vast ocean. She wanted to dance and sing and feel the sand; and to grieve, and long, and love.

This is the great *Lila* of our existence on Earth.

CHAPTER 16

Your Story

It is the task of the enlightened not only to ascend to learning and to see the good but to be willing to descend again to those prisoners and to share their troubles and their honors, whether they are worth having or not.

~ Plato, "The Allegory of the Cave"

...

We have hope. Rebellions are built on hope.

~ Jyn Erson, <u>Rogue One</u>

Undertake your quest.

Enter into your cave of darkness, battle your elusive tigers, confront the Dark Side of the Force and then uncover the hidden treasures of *your* soul.

That is sort of the point of this book, in case you missed it. I wanted to share parts of my journey and what it taught me, in the hope that it might be helpful to you on your journey.

And your quest is guaranteed to look different than mine, and your personal truths might be different from, or in apparent opposition to, my truths. Nothing is black or white to a true yogi or Jedi.

It is not my intention to convince you that what is true for me should also be true for you; my intention is to get you to find *your* Truth and to become an integrated, more whole version of You.

Go on your quest.

Find your personal Groundhog Day dramas and solve them.

Confront your own anger demon, or whatever your personal tiger might be, and integrate its wisdom. Come up against the dark side of the Force and emerge a Jedi. Figure out your story and own it, so that you may co-create the ending. Experience the full range of human emotion and fully commit to your role in this Earth-play.

The World is in desperate need of humans that are ready to step into their own herodom and undertake their personal quests.

This is especially true in first world countries, like America, where we mostly don't have to worry about basic necessities like clean water, food, and shelter.[34] In fact, as folks whose basic needs are met, we have a *responsibility* to awaken to our highest Selves and to help dissipate the world's problems in the highest and most unifying ways.

Be on Team Minerva and resolve to start your journey from right where you are right now, with all of your perceived faults and vices, and while you live out your seemingly mundane existence.

Remember that Minerva is the Roman warrior goddess; she embodies wisdom, the arts, and strategic warfare.

As we embark on our personal quests for truth, we can evoke Minerva and undertake an inner battle with wisdom, creativity and courage. We can choose to face and integrate our shadow.

And we don't have to be perfect or deny our humanity while we do it. That isn't the point. We are allowed to be a little "rotten," "naughty," "sinful," or "unruly." We

---

[34] Sadly this isn't true for all Americans, and we really have to work together to find innovative solutions. All human beings deserve to have their basic needs met.

start where we are, and we learn and grow through our journeys.

So be an unruly warrior and embark on *your* spiritual quest for freedom!

You can undertake practices like devotion, yoga *asana*, *pratyahara*, *tapas*, *svadhyaya*, walks in nature, mindfulness meditation, music lessons, art, writing, and mini-quests like the ones in this book, to help bring yourself into a state of receptivity.

You can start to notice signs and coincidences and symbols and songs and movie metaphors in your day-to-day life. You can start to look inward, rather than outward, when you feel anger, and start to unravel and solve your own personal Groundhog-Day-like mysteries.

And we can all strive to recognize the anguish and frustration felt by our sleeping brothers and sisters, who might lash out at us and others in acts of hate. We can respond to those acts of hate with fierce grace, admonishing the act while feeling compassion for the actor.

Like the Aesop's Fable about the North Wind and Sun:

The North Wind and the Sun had a quarrel about which of them was the stronger. While they were disputing with much heat and bluster, a Traveler passed along the road wrapped in a cloak.

"Let us agree," said the Sun, "that he is the stronger who can strip that Traveler of his cloak."

"Very well," growled the North Wind, and at once sent a cold, howling blast against the Traveler.

With the first gust of wind the ends of the cloak whipped about the Traveler's body. But he immediately wrapped it closely around him, and the harder the Wind blew, the tighter he held it to him. The North Wind tore angrily at the cloak, but all his efforts were in vain.

Then the Sun began to shine. At first his beams were gentle, and in the pleasant warmth after the bitter cold of the North Wind, the Traveler unfastened his cloak and let it hang loosely from his shoulders. The Sun's rays grew warmer and warmer. The man took off his cap and mopped his brow. At last he became so heated that he pulled off his cloak, and, to escape the blazing sunshine, threw himself down in the welcome shade of a tree by the roadside.

We can slowly, but surely, and patiently, uplift humanity into its divine birthright. Not by force or coercion but by shining brightly like the sun and by being living examples of authenticity, love and compassion.

So, undertake your journey.

Go on your quest.

Enter into your cave of darkness, confront your own personal tigers and emerge victorious—as an authentic embodiment of You, living your Truth with love, authenticity, and freedom.

CONCLUSION

Or is it?

Do our journeys really ever come to an end?

Mine has not. And if you are a savvy reader, you might have noticed on the title page that this book is a "Part One."

That means there is a Part Two.

So if you felt like you wanted more, like there were some stories left open-ended, some experiences I could have delved deeper into, or you just plain want more of me, you are in luck!

Stay tuned for Rotten Minerva, Part Two: Really Rotten Minerva, where I will fill in some gaps, give you more of my personal experiences, and provide my unqualified opinion on even more important topics.

You're welcome.

See you soon.

Quests

(aka "Mini Quests")

> Quest: *"an act or instance of seeking; a pursuit or search."*

The following "mini-quests" are small "acts of seeking" that can be incorporated into your day-to-day life. They can be a part of your larger Quest for self-discovery.

These mini-quest practices are designed to bring you closer to your highest self and in alignment with the present moment, so that you can fully utilize your intuition and instincts. They have personally helped me on my journey.

With these tools and others that you will no doubt discover on your own during your journey, it is my hope that you will feel the bliss that comes with aligning with your soul.

Oak Quest

Channel your inner oak tree

In the "We are Family" Chapter, we discussed Ram Dass' suggestion that humans are like trees and that we should practice treating them that way: appreciating them for who they are.

Another useful tool, is to turn yourself into a tree. Trees have a great wisdom. They are some of the oldest living things on Earth. Some of them have quietly weathered and witnessed dramatic shifts in human history.

They embody a silent steadiness and knowing, mixed with kindness and generosity. Think of Shel Silverstein's "Giving Tree." I find this especially true with large trees like redwoods or oaks. And trees are directly responsible for the air that we breathe, making them deeply connected to us.

Sometimes if I am in a place of waiting, or in a group of people where I feel a bit awkward or uncomfortable, I imagine that I am a boundless oak tree. I feel my legs ground deep into the earth as if rooted there. If I am sitting, I move forward in my seat so that my feet connect with the ground. I sit up straight or stand tall and put my attention into my body.

I try to embody the quiet understanding and kindness of the tree: just being there and allowing everyone else in the room to be there too.

Try this mini-quest for yourself and experiment with your own inner tree wisdom.

Steel Quest

Embody protection and healthy boundaries while living open-heartedly

As someone who feels sensitive to other people's "stuff," I often feel social anxiety and uneasiness in large crowds. I have found that using the metaphor of "steel" (and also amethyst) has helped me to remain open-hearted and loving while using caution and employing boundaries.

The symbolic use of steel has also helped me to literally maintain better boundaries in my relationships with other humans when necessary, while at the same time offering love and compassion. It is sometimes difficult to find that balance, but it is important that we do so. I have found that starting on the symbolic level often leads to real-life shifts.

Steel is symbolic of strength and protection. That is why Superman is the "man of steel." We can channel our inner superhero with the imagery of steel.

The Steel mini-quest goes like this: I imagine a barrier of steel around my body.

I envision that lower frequency emotions—like anger and fear—are impervious to my body of steel. At the same time, the green light of my heart chakra shines right through the steel armor like Iron Man's Arc Reactor. I am not withholding my love and light.

Amethyst imagery also works for me. Amethyst is a beautiful, protective, violet-colored gemstone. I imagine a layer of it surrounds my body. Sometimes I even combine the steel and the amethyst tools together.

With the help of this imagery, I feel protected and safe in sharing and witnessing the love with my fellow humans. I feel that I am able to maintain boundaries and caution while living with an open heart.

Try this mini-quest and observe for yourself the utility of steel (and amethyst!) as a symbol of strength and protection.

Cross Quest

Notice signs and symbols like crosses as validation on the Quest

Crosses are highly symbolic; they symbolize a cross-roads: a point of transition from one phase of life to another.

And for those who have a Christian religious heritage, they symbolize Jesus Christ, whose life itself invites us to transition from an ego-centric existence to a divine-centered one.

Looking for and seeing crosses as signs of validation on the quest is a fun starting point into the world of symbols, metaphors, and magical coincidences.

We discussed looking for signs in the Film Appreciation Chapter. And signs can be anything that has special meaning for you. If you are looking for a place to get started with seeing signs and symbols, crosses can be a great launching point.

Crosses are everywhere. They can be both literal crosses that are clearly set up in reverence to Jesus, or things like telephone poles, sticks, and bookshelf framing that look like a cross.

Start with the intention to see crosses. It could be as simple as reading this mini-quest and consciously deciding to be open to seeing them yourself. If you want you can take a moment, wherever you are, to see what crosses are within eyeshot. Maybe there is one in the way the cabinets meet in the kitchen, or in the tiles on the floor.

I noticed that once I set my intention to see crosses, I started to see them often, and mostly when I was not looking for them at all. Sometimes while I am driving and deep in thought, my eyes will drift to a cross by the roadside that seems to have been placed there at just the right moment, as if in response to my silent thought.

When that happens, it feels like a validation of my quest, and serves to lessen the hold of my doubts and fears.

Experiment with crosses and other signs and symbols for yourself, and see if they help to confirm and validate your path.

Mosquito Quest

Align with the wisdom of the insect realm

We often think of insects, especially mosquitos, as pests.

But like the cedar tree I talked about in the "Magic is Magic" Chapter, they can be befriended. And what sweet friends they make!

(For serious.)

My own relationship with insects has not always been friendly. I was someone who often complained that mosquitos seemed to single me out and bite me even when others around me went by unscathed.

But like all animals that we encounter on a daily basis, there is often a deeper meaning. Like the Carl Jung scarab beetle story we discussed in the Film Appreciation Chapter, even insects can be divine messengers.

It might be easier to connect with insects like beetles or ladybugs, so start there. Both are highly symbolic. Ladybugs, for example, are associated with luck and abundance. If one flies into your life, take notice.

And if you can connect with ladybugs or beetles, maybe you can slowly start to connect with other insects that wander across your path daily, like ants and spiders and mosquitos. They are all highly symbolic too. Mosquitos symbolize agitation, persistence, discovery and release.

Try this to start: the next time an insect wanders into your path, resist the urge to kill it or run from it. Take a moment and speak to it, silently or out loud. Say something like, "hello, little friend, what are you here to teach me today?" In the simple act you are taking a moment to recognize the divinity in that bug, and see it as something larger than its "pesky" nature.

I've found that since I started befriending individual insects, that the insect realm as a whole understood the message, much like my experience with the cedar tree.

Try it for yourself and see what happens when you start to see and treat insects a little differently.

Sun Quest

Show reverence to the sun as a symbol of Life

The sun is responsible for all of life on Earth.

Without it, our lives on Earth would not be possible. That is why ancient cultures worshipped a "sun" god. And it is no coincidence that Jesus is the "son" of God, a homophone for "sun."

The sun is what makes plants grow, through the process of photosynthesis. And humans can experience a sort of photosynthesis for themselves. It is said that some great yogis have been able to live on prana from the sun alone, and forego any food.

I like to show reverence for the sun daily, as a way to align myself with Nature and Life. I start with a sun-centered practice usually first thing in the morning, and throughout the day when I remember.

My typical morning practices are to sing the Gayatri Mantra, a beautiful devotion song to the sun; or to practice *surya namaskara,* also known as sun salutations, a yoga asana sequence. There are guided videos for both the Gayatri Mantra and the sun salutations on TheYogaLawyer YouTube Channel.

But even taking a moment to close your eyes and feel the warmth and greatness of the sun is itself an act of gratitude to Nature.

Incorporating moments like this into your day-to-day life is a meaningful way to show gratitude and reverence for the sun as a metaphor for our own divine nature.

Yes/No Quest

Tune in to your inner wisdom when faced with indecision.

In Chapter 10, "Magic is Magic," we talked about tuning into our innate inner wisdom. I'm talking about that heart-yes that can act as confirmation when we are faced with indecision.

Here is a simple way to set the stage for accessing that wisdom.

First, sit comfortably, preferably with straight spine and feet on the floor. Take a few deep inhales and exhales to bring yourself into the moment.

Then ask yourself a question that has a clear, unequivocal no for you. It is often easier to start with no. An example would be, "should I judge myself harshly right now?" The answer to that question should clearly be no, because it is just about never correct to harshly judge anyone, including oneself. If that one doesn't connect, sometimes I recommend, "would it be smart to set myself on fire right now?" But that one can sometimes provoke a strong, full-body, "no" that is uncomfortable.

The point is to pick a question with an answer that is a clear "no" for you.

Then sit with the answer. Feel what "no" feels like to your body. You might feel sensations anywhere in your body. I sometimes feel tingling in my arms and legs. Or maybe you feel nothing at all. The point is to notice.

Now try a yes. What is a question that has an easy yes answer to you? Maybe something like, "Should I be exactly where I am at the present moment?" I've found the answer to that question is almost always yes for almost everyone. Or try something associated with a commitment that you already know you must keep like, "is it a good idea to pick up my kids from school today?"

The answer to the hypothetical should be a clear yes for you. Then sit with what "yes" feels like to your body. Notice any sensations, particularly around the area of your heart or belly. Yes might be a stronger sensation than no or vice versa. Compare what the two responses feel like for you.

By practicing identifying what a clear "yes" or "no" feels like for you, you can sort of "calibrate" your body so that it is ready when faced with true indecision.

I use this tool very often when making decisions as simple as what to order from the menu, to those more complicated—like whether or not to take on a new legal case. I do not abandon logic and reason, but I give my heart-yes as much credibility as my logical brain when I am wrestling with a choice. I've found with practice, that the two are almost never at odds with each other, and that my life flows with grace and ease when I live from my heart.

Undertake the Yes/No mini-quest for yourself and bring to light your heart's ever-present wisdom.

Mantra Quest

Harness the power of mantras as a doorway into meditative states

I often hear feedback from yoga students that meditating is very difficult because they just can't "quiet their minds."

A couple things about that: first, remember from "The Real Yoga" Chapter that quieting the mind might not be the point—yoga is more about stilling the unconscious waves of thought than completely silencing the mind.

But maybe more importantly, meditating is hard if your approach is to try to sit still and not think; or even to sit still and focus on the breath.

I find it much easier to focus on a mantra, which can be repeated out loud or silently. The practice goes like this: I sit down to practice and start repeating my mantra; any time I notice that my mind has gotten caught up in a thought, I bring it back to the mantra, which I repeat over and over again until the practice is over.

The Sanskrit word, "mantra" literally translates as "mind-protecting."

Not only do Sanskrit mantras help to "protect the mind" from unconscious thought waves, but their use also has physical benefits. In fact, a recent peer-reviewed study confirmed through MRI tests that chanting "OM" stimulates the vagus nerve, which is associated with heart function and digestion.[35] Stimulation of the vagus nerve is a treatment for depression and epilepsy, and has many other health benefits.

OM is a great simple mantra to get started with. There are also longer mantras, like "Om Namah Shivaya" which translates to "I bow to the divinity in me."

But my favorite type of mantra meditation practice is the practice of bhajan, which is the devotional singing of mantras.

Amma says this about bhajan: "To gain concentration during this dark age, devotional singing is better than meditation. Through intense singing, other distracting sounds will be overcome, and concentration will be achieved."

I find that her words are true for me. I spend a few minutes each morning singing devotional yoga mantras

---

35 Kalyani, B; Venkatasubramanian, Ganesan; et al., Int J Yoga,; 4(1): 3–6 (Jan-Jun 2011)

and I instantly feel uplifted and my mind is calmed without effort.

Some of my favorite mantras to sing are the Gayatri Mantra and the Hanuman Chalisa. They are both widely available on the interwebs. Also, there are many guided mantra practices on my website theyogalawyer.com and on TheYogaLawyer You Tube Channel.

Try mantra practice for yourself and experience the physical, mental, and spiritual benefits it brings.

Asana Quest

Use your asana practice as a form of tapas (purification)

Yoga asana can be a useful form of internal purification when the focus shifts from the external teacher to the internal one.

I talk about my own experiences with tapas and the magic that can come with purifying practices in the "Magic is Magic" Chapter. For me it came as a direct result of my Mysore-style Ashtanga Yoga asana practice.

Beneficial asana practice should include the use of the breath and the bandhas (internal locks). The point is to have an inner point of focus so that the practice becomes a moving meditation. Find a teacher and research the use of breath and internal locks if they are not already part of your practice. That is the first step to treating your yoga exercise as tapas.

In addition, the following light imagery exercise can be incorporated as part of your regular asana practice, which can be as simple as performing 3 sun salutations or as elaborate as a 2-hour sequence. Try adding it to your practice for a week or more and notice any effects. It is especially helpful when feeling inflamed.

It goes like this: on your inhalations, breath in a clear, bright, blue light.

See the blue light travel throughout the body and particularly into any areas that want attention. Imagine it mixing with any red inflammation in your body so that all of your body fills with blue light.

Then, on your exhalations, breath out vivid red light.

Imagine that any and all inflammation is leaving the body. The body is healthy and balanced, calm and cool. Try it and see the effects in your own body. And tell me about it, if you like! I always welcome feedback. Namaste

Glossary of Yogic (Sanskrit) Terms

Asana - refers to the physical postures.

Ashtanga Yoga – originally refers to Patanjali's eight limbs of yoga practices. "Ashtanga" means "eight limbs." However, the term "Ashtanga Yoga" is also used to characterize the intense form of _asana_ practice popularized by Shri K. Pattabhi Jois, which is still taught by his daughter, Saraswathi, and grandson, Sharath, in Mysore, Karnataka, India.

Bhajan - devotional form of meditation, where one chants or sings Sanskrit yoga mantras.

Bhakta – a devotee; a bhakti yoga practitioner.

Bhakti – —he practice of devotion or _Ishvara pranidhana_.

Dharma – your duty or soul purpose.

Ishvara pranidhana – devotion to your personal concept of the divine.

Karma – action or "cause and effect." Karma can result from current or past desires. Karma can also be thought of like this: whatever you sow you will reap. Plant "anger" seeds and reap more anger; plant love seeds and reap more love.

Karma yoga - selfless action or service.

Lila – The creative play of God.

Nirodha – Calming; literally translates as "without Rudra," the god of storms.

Niyamas – Moral practices including cleanliness, self-study, and devotion.

Pada – literally translates to "foot" or "step." Can refer to a chapter of a book with four parts.

Prana – life force; breath.

Pranayama - yogic breathing practices.

Pratyahara - sense withdrawal; also refers to the inner exploration of emotions.

Samadhi - supreme bliss or super consciousness.

Svadhyaya – self-study.

Tapas – purification practices.

Yamas - moral observances like truth, non-stealing, non-grasping, and non-harming.

Yogi – one who is dedicated to the spiritual quest; aka Jedi; As Krishna said to Arjuna in the Bhagavad Gita, "The yogi rises above the ascetics, those with psychic knowledge, and even those who do meritorious works. Therefore, Arjuna, be a yogi!"

ABOUT THE AUTHOR

For many years, Kelli Hastings led a very material-minded, anxiety-ridden existence and worked long hours as an attorney.

In 2010, three weeks after her son was born, her younger brother died of Hodgkin's Lymphoma. Her father died of lung cancer six months to the day after her brother.

These personal tragedies sparked within her a re-awakening. Her journey led her deeper into the practice and study of Yoga, and then to India.

Kelli spent about six months total in India, over the course of 3 years. She brought her young son with her each time; he was only 20 months old their first trip. In India, Kelli connected to and felt deeply the Love that permeates all of existence. It transformed her and set her life on a different trajectory.

She continues to maintain a part-time solo law practice and owns a sensory deprivation floating and yoga center in Central Florida. She is driven by an inner connection to divinity and hopes that by living her life openly and honestly that she might inspire others to undertake their own inward journey toward authenticity and freedom; and ultimately to connect deeply to the Love that resides in each of our hearts.

To find out what Kelli is up to, check out her website, theyogalawyer.com.